On God's Radar

On God's Radar

MY WALK ACROSS AMERICA

Robert Schoen

Stone Bridge Press · Berkeley, California

This book is dedicated to the memory of my father, Michael W. Schoen. He was always there for me, even after he was gone.

Published by
Stone Bridge Press
P. O. Box 8208, Berkeley, CA 94707
TEL 510-524-8732 · sbp@stonebridge.com · www.stonebridge.com

Author photograph on page 208 by James & Pamela Au Photography.

Cover design and book layout by Linda Ronan.

Printed in the United States of America.

10 9 8 7 6 5 4 3 2 1   2023 2022 2021 2020 2019

p-ISBN: 978-1-61172-053-2

Contents

Why Are You Doing This?

I lost track of how many times I was asked this question as I walked 2,644 miles across America, coast-to-coast, in 2017 and 2018.*

The question is legitimate. Most of the time when I was asked the question I was walking or eating a meal or tired after a long day, and I just didn't have the time or energy to deal with it. So here's the answer I'd give:

My Dad passed away last year at 96. He was a World War II veteran, and I'm walking in honor of his memory.

Each person would respond with an understanding smile, a nod, occasionally an embrace, and often a "God Bless You" or other remark that reflected approval. *Here is a son who honors his father. (Probably his mother, too.)*

My answer never failed to satisfy anyone's curiosity. *Never.* And no one questioned me further. I wonder about this for a couple of reasons.

First, it doesn't really answer the question.

Second, while I certainly *do* honor the memory of my father and think of him more now than I ever did while he was alive, it's not the reason I walked. In fact, my dad died just a month before I began the incredible journey that took me through 14 states in 170 days.

The truth as to why I did this is personal. It speaks to a selfish desire and is more about me than anything or anyone else.

I walked across the country because I wanted to do something that most people don't do.

* The second most-asked question was, "How many pairs of shoes did you go through?" I still get asked this regularly, and the answer is maybe five or six—I lost track. But who gives a damn?

That's it. Simple. Easy. Straightforward. The truth. But it's not an answer that's apt to gain the approval or affirmation of strangers along the highway. Or waitresses at IHOP or folks standing behind a counter at the Dollar store, Burger King, a convenience store, or the front desk at a Motel 6 or Holiday Inn. No one is going to hear this answer and say, "God Bless You!"

Ask me if I care. I don't. Although I did dedicate this walk to my father, I did not attempt or complete this journey for anyone except myself. It was a personal goal, a quest, a journey for its own sake, and in the end a personal achievement. My walking over 2,600 miles did not fund any charitable cause. I did it for me.

But that said, I did not do it alone. I had help all along the way. A lot of support. And I learned many things—about humanity, about nature, about my country, about inner strength and self-motivation, and about overcoming obstacles. I learned about giving and accepting, and about what I believe is significant and what is not.

In the end, however, the two most important things I learned had to do with the goodness of people and my own belief in what, for lack of a better description, term, or name, I'll call God.

This was a personal journey that I shared with a thousand people. The power of social media was not lost on me, and I faithfully recorded *something* every day. As a result, I became aware of the significance of my successes and failures, as well as the realization that friends, family members, acquaintances, and strangers were not just observing my progress; they were also worrying about me, rooting me on, and very often praying for me.

I was alone, but I was not alone. And I was never lonely. It's just not in my nature, and I've come to learn why.

It's because I've lived my life *On God's Radar*.

Oakland, California

The Night Before . . .

YOU ARE NEVER TOO OLD TO SET ANOTHER GOAL OR TO DREAM A NEW DREAM

– C.S. Lewis

It's the night before Day One. Sharon and I drove down from Oakland to Huntington Beach in a Toyota 4Runner rental, which we just dropped off at John Wayne Airport.

The traffic coming down was smooth except for a few Easter Sunday fender-benders. The Runabout kart is packed, and tomorrow morning after breakfast I'll get my feet wet in the Pacific. Then I'll take that single step that begins my longest journey.

Santa Ana River Trail, Huntington Beach, California

Day 1

This morning I waded into the Pacific Ocean, beginning a journey such as I've never taken before.

I was joined at the foot of the Santa Ana River Trail by my wife, Sharon Chabon, and my longtime friend and colleague, Dr. Bronson Hamada, who lives and works in Huntington Beach and walked the first few miles with me.

As I walked along the trail, I witnessed the sad spectacle of many homeless people—men, women, and children—living in over a thousand tents.

I've only been walking a day and I've already seen a week's worth of stuff. After 18 miles, my legs were not happy! But I did manage to finish the long first day of my journey successfully.

Day 2   *Anaheim, California*

"What's in the box?" I asked the man from California Fish and Wildlife. He was on a ladder, inspecting a large birdhouse attached to a tree. The 36 boxes along the trail are meant to house wood ducks, and each box was being checked for eggs. This particular box had 18 eggs in it!

The Santa Ana River Trail is under major construction, with detours and blocked paths everywhere I walked. I took a long detour in Yorba Linda, but had to double back when it led in the wrong direction.

When the Santa Ana River contains water, water fowl, and jumping fish, it's certainly a beautiful sight. But much of the trail, mostly built in the mid-1990s, is less romantic than the name suggests, and I spent much of this very beautiful day walking along freeways and construction sites.

Ontario, California   Days 3–4

Cars, Construction, and Cows. That describes today's walk.

This was supposed to be an "easy" 16-mile day, 70% of it on sidewalks. Sadly, the other 30% was hell and frustration, with a sidewalk suddenly ending at a sandy side path or a busy highway with no shoulder.

At one point, I had to lug my kart up a small hill.

My legs are really sore, and I've decided to name the kart "Walker," because that's what it's been serving as.

I've decided to take a day off and give my legs, knees, feet, and toes a break. The Jacuzzi was great!

Day 5   *Fontana, California*

Haven Avenue was anything but a haven as I struggled to get past Ontario airport. Finally I reached Arrow Route, a very pleasant street, which led me to historic Route 66.

After a frustrating hour of backtracking, I finally reached the Pacific Electric Trail, a wide, paved bike path that was just a joy to walk on.

At a Tijuana-style taco restaurant on Foothill Boulevard that's being rebuilt, I waved to a man in the doorway. He motioned me over, and after learning about my walk, Gustavo invited me to stay the night on his property.

I fell asleep in my tent to a strange mix of sounds: trucks and motorcycles, crickets, birds, barking dogs, and Mexican music.

San Bernardino, California

Day 6

In spite of the tuba bass lines and staccato accordion fills that went on until 2:30 in the morning, my day began at 5 a.m.

I broke "camp" and was at the IHOP at 7 a.m. when it opened. My waitperson was very sweet and allowed me to charge my phone in the kitchen. But I really did *not* order the ham omelet! (A note on my diet and eating habits: Although I do eat fish, I haven't eaten meat, poultry, or shellfish for decades.)

I followed the Pacific Electric Trail until it ended and then took a side trip to the FedEx office where I sent home over 9 pounds of stuff.

The lady at the front desk of the Motel 6 put me in a handicapped room. She must have observed how I was limping and leaning on Walker (my kart).

Day 7

Fisherman's Retreat, Redlands, California

San Timoteo Creek bike path was great to walk on, but San Timoteo Canyon Rd. was a two-lane blacktop that called for constant vigilance in the traffic.

My left knee was complaining when I spied *Fisherman's Retreat,* an RV park filled with vacationing families, dogs, and a woman wandering around calling, "Sarah, here kitty!"

I paid the "non-member" price for an RV spot and pitched my tent on the grass. I was eating a cod sandwich and cole slaw at the café when Karen, the owner, told me about a woman who'd come through a few weeks before on a cross-country walk. Her name was Jeannette and, unlike me, she was "Walking for Purity."

I chatted with a Canadian guy in the RV behind me while he smoked a cigarette and his two small dogs peed. He said, "If you're hungry, I'm just putting some pork chops on the grill." I thanked him and said I'd already eaten.

Banning, California   Day 8

Today was probably the best day I've had on the road so far. My blisters are disappearing and I was having no knee or foot pain. The weather was cool, in the mid-50°s to -60°s, and the sun stayed behind clouds.

Crossing into Beaumont, I encountered a WIDE sidewalk. So no need to dodge oncoming traffic for a while as I enjoyed the sights and sounds around me—freight trains, a jackrabbit with a very white tail, and a large field filled with so many different bird songs that it sounded like an orchestra.

I stopped for lunch at Subway, one of my favorite restaurants. It's a good place to get the vegetables I crave but often can't find on the road.

At my motel, I spoke on the phone with a long-distance cyclist. Although he wound up giving me misinformation, he meant well. The cycling lobby is responsible for designated bike lanes in many cities and states. Often this is a veritable life-saver.

Day 9   *White Water, California*

Today was a 14-mile, frustrating day. The billboard tells it all.

In order to avoid the Morongo Indian Reservation (you can drive through the reservation, but you can't walk through it), I followed complicated directions given to me by three different people. But navigating the railroad tracks south of the Interstate Highway was complicated.

At one point the road ended abruptly, but then continued on the other side of the railroad tracks. Fortunately I was strong enough (thanks to pull-ups and push-ups) to lug my gear up the gravel-track side and over four rails to the other side. It took me three trips.

Fighting gusty winds and exhausted, I eventually pitched my tent in an empty lot.

Morongo Valley, California

Day 10

If today had been Day 1, I am not sure there would have been a Day 2.

At 6 a.m., walking into a beautiful sunrise, it was sand and more sand. Two hours later I finally reached an asphalt pavement and thought my troubles were over as I walked up a hill that would take

me around the I-10 Freeway. But a service crew informed me I was in a restricted area and directed me to "16th Avenue," yet *another* dirt road! Hours later I reached Route 62 (Twentynine Palms Hwy). Hallelujah! As I climbed up and up, the path became narrower and the traffic heavier.

On reaching Morongo Valley, I entered the Monument Bar & Grill where I met Chad, John, Juan, and Bill—all great guys— and bought a round of beer for everyone. Bill invited me to camp in his backyard overnight.

Day 11   *Joshua Tree, California*

In the morning, I packed up my gear, said goodbye to Bill, and headed toward Yucca Valley.

My dear friend, author Alice Camille, had set up an introduction for me at St. Mary of the Valley church. Mary, the administrative assistant (not the saint), informed me that Father Mark Bertelli and the church, in an expression of hospitality, wanted to put me up at a nearby hotel of my choice.

I accepted their gift graciously and gratefully, and chose a motel in Joshua Tree.

Today's walk was a delight. The road had wide shoulders and I saw some beautiful flowers along the way. (I did *not* stop in at the shooting gallery.)

Twentynine Palms, Days 12–13
California

I was out the door of the High Desert Inn in Joshua Tree at 6 a.m. and checked into Motel 6 in Twentynine Palms five hours later.

Along the way I spotted a bench under a shady porch of the New Testament Baptist Church. While I rested, no one (New Testament *or* Old Testament) disturbed me.

Dayle at the Motel 6 allowed me to check in early. I ate lunch at the Del Taco next door and then took a well-deserved nap.

For dinner, I took a short two-mile walk to Subway where I picked up a foot-long tuna sub. Then two miles back.

Today was a good day.

Day 14

Wonder Valley, California

Today was the first day I walked 20 miles intentionally and without any particular pain. Since I'd started walking at 5:40 a.m., I was ready to quit for the day and set up my tent by 2:20 p.m. I'd put in a good day.

At about 11 a.m. a man jogged by and waved. Returning a little while later, he walked with me and asked what I was doing. His name was George and he was a firefighter at the Wonder Valley station.

As I sat down at a nearby picnic table in the shade to eat lunch, a man drove up and got out of his Jeep to say hello and said he'd seen me struggling up the treacherous hill to Morongo Valley a few days before. Bernie and I had a nice chat, and he offered me a bottle of water, which I accepted, even though I have four gallons of water in my kart. Bernie is an example of one of the "angels" I continue to encounter on my journey.

I'm camped behind some bushes, 100 feet off of Amboy Road, and can still hear the light traffic I've been listening to since day one. For dinner tonight, I have peanut butter, two kinds of crackers, and a banana. (Did you know there are more calories, calories from fat, total fat, sodium, and sugar in a serving of Nabisco Wheat Thins than in a serving of Triscuits?)

Amboy Road, California **Day 15**

As I got near the top of an ascent, I met Linda, who did a U-turn and waited for me to approach. "I made you some sandwiches." I turned down the two ham sandwiches, but graciously accepted four tangerines. "When you reach those two cell towers up there, it's all downhill."

Soon, there she was again after driving home for more tangerines, carrots, and a zucchini. "Linda, how can I ever repay you?"

"You can't." And then, like the Lone Ranger, she was gone.

Two hours later Dave pulled up and said he was a friend of Chad, whom I'd met at the bar in Morongo Valley. We sat in his air-conditioned car and I cooled off.

Later on, a 40-ish guy driving a BMW convertible and sporting a Hollywood haircut had to slow to a stop near me—because of oncoming traffic, he would have hit me otherwise. He gave me a disgusted look. *See? You made me slow down!* For the next 10 minutes I kept up an imaginary conversation with that guy in my head. *What a jerk.* As I was stewing, a tattooed guy with a shaved head pulled up in a white Chevy pickup and passed me a cold bottle of water before he sped away.

Virtually every driver—truckers, bikers, dudes in pickup trucks, men and women, young and old—responds to my wave with a wave of their own.

John and Vickie from Cloverdale handed me some cash: "Buy yourself a beer!" An older woman said, "God bless you," gave me some water, and drove away.

Another day filled with angels.

Day 16

Roy's Motel and Café, Amboy, California

With the temperature over 102°, I was already tired at 6 a.m. as I pushed toward Amboy and Roy's Gasoline. Once again Linda pulled up in her little white car. She's a voluble, blonde Mama Cass in a floppy leather hat, an extra large leopard skin muumuu top, and no shoes. She brought more tangerines, carrots, bottles of water, and a green pepper.

At Roy's I bought a Route 66 root beer and a Snickers, and I sat in the shade out front for six long hours, waiting for the day to cool off. I spoke with French-Canadians, Brits, Germans, a Swiss guy, Virginia (from Buffalo but now living in Norway), and Zach, who as a teenager used to visit the nearby Amboy Crater after buying a Coke at Roy's for a nickel.

At 5 p.m. I walked a mile before camping. The heat done me in.

Cadiz, National Trails Hwy, California

Day 17

In spite of a 5:10 a.m. start, five hours later the heat had defeated me.

I'd been walking on old Route 66. Some of the bridges are being repaired, so it's closed to regular traffic.

Scott McGaha drove up in a large truck and asked how I was doing. Later Dave, driving a Caterpillar tractor, gave me a bottle of water.

Scott soon returned with water, Gatorade, and Granola bars and invited me to use his trailer. "The AC is on and the door's open." I staggered into his Jayco trailer, took off my shoes and shirt, and collapsed across the foot of his bed.

When he returned a little while later, he said, "You know, if you're going to walk across the Mojave, you should do it at night."

Day 18   *Cadiz, California*

I took Scott's advice and left his air-conditioned trailer at 7:45 p.m.

After walking two-and-a-half hours up the hill, I was exhausted and set up camp on the side of the road. At 6 a.m. in the morning I resumed walking. Descending down a steep hill, it soon became too hot to continue, and I pitched my tent in the shade under one of the bridges, where dates of 1934 and 1939 were painted on the joists above me.

I ate, drank, and waited. After sundown I packed up my gear and walked less than a mile before realizing I did not have the strength to go on.

I called Scott for help. He picked me up, drove me to his trailer, fed me canned chicken and dumpling soup, and set me up for the night on the convertible bench seating/sleeping unit. (It was the first time I'd eaten chicken in 25 years; but I needed the protein and nutrients, fast.) Before falling asleep, I managed to write a blog post about my day.

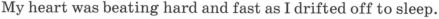

Kingman, Arizona Days 19–20

My heart was beating hard and fast as I drifted off to sleep.

When he left for work at 5 a.m., Scott knew I wasn't in good shape. He asked if he could take me somewhere. But my plan was to rest and try again Monday morning.

Several hours later someone knocked on the door. *"Dr. Schoen?"* What the hell! In walked Deanna, a long-time patient, friend, and artist (she designed Sharon's and my Ketubah, our Jewish wedding contract). With her was her spouse, Walter, a retired psychiatrist.

Deanna explained that as they followed me online, they decided I needed help. They'd driven hours and cleverly located Scott's Jayco trailer, hoping to assist me.

We sat in their rented SUV with the AC on, and ate from the wonderful selection of food they'd brought. It was decision time. I called my wife and mentors for advice, and we all agreed—the desert was going to kill me, and it had already started. Scott came by and he too agreed.

The temperature in nearby Needles was 102° as we lifted Walker into the SUV and headed to Kingman, Arizona.

How could I ever repay the incredible gifts of caring and intervention I'd received from these angels?

Today was a day of rest, and I needed it. I ate, drank, and napped. Repeat. Repeat again.

I also did laundry, dipped in the cold pool, and pondered my self-inflicted circumstances. After posting my decision, I received nothing

but support from my communities of friends, family, and walkers. Certainly I'm disappointed; but I am also alive to walk another day. When I complained online that my walk would no longer be considered a "pure" coast-to-coast walk, Cousin Naomi famously responded, *"Pure, Shmure!"* Since she's Canadian and very smart, I respect her opinion.

Day 21   *Route 66, Arizona*

After two nights at Motel 6, I picked up some egg sandwiches at Carl's Junior and resumed my walk on Historic Route 66 at 7:30 a.m. *It is cold!* I was wearing an extra shirt and gloves.

Walking through Kingman, this portion of Route 66 is also known as Andy Devine Avenue, so I looked it up. Andy Devine grew up in Kingman and achieved familiarity as a result of his role as Guy Madison's sidekick in the Wild Bill Hickok TV show and his own children's show in the late 1950s. But his career in film, television, and theater is also quite impressive.

As I walked, I enjoyed the hundreds of vintage cars—and vintage people—participating in the "Historic Route 66 Fun Run."

Later, I camped between the highway and the railroad tracks near the Valle Vista golf course. (Too bad I didn't bring my clubs.)

Crozier, Arizona   Day 22

Arizona is beautiful, reminiscent of the TV Westerns I watched as a boy, typically mounted on a green leather hassock (my saddle) atop a dining room chair (my horse) in front of my grandmother's small screen television. The good guy would shoot the gun out of the bad guy's hand. Or he'd ride his horse alongside the bad guy's horse; they'd fall off together and have a short fight ending in Hopalong (or Gene or Roy) saving the day.

Now I am surrounded by those same vistas. I climb hills, dodge speeding vehicles, watch endless freight trains go by, and long to reach the next town.

This morning I met Rory, 32, cycling from LA to the East Coast, looking to find meaning in his life. Later, at Hackberry, I chatted with some Dutch tourists (in Dutch my name means "shoe").

The many Route 66 ghost towns are a mixture of old rusted cars, schlock, kitsch, convenience stores, and Grand Canyon tourists. Today I encountered a leather-clad French tour group riding Harleys. *Mais oui.*

I rested near the Bureau of Indian Affairs and later set up my tent near the town of Crozier. In spite of the cars, trucks, and trains, it's peaceful lying in my tent, just waiting for the sun to go down.

The Beginning

At age 70, I was retired, in good health, and leading a full, comfortable life. But I was restless.

I wanted to do something that most people do not do.

Travel to the moon? Nah. Too expensive. Climb Mount Everest? Too cold, not enough O_2. Kayak across the Pacific Ocean? Too wet. Swim from Cuba to Florida? It's already been done, and I try to avoid sharks whenever possible.

I needed something within reason.

Ever since reading Peter Jenkins' 1979 book, *A Walk Across America,* I'd thought about walking coast-to-coast. I did some research, read several books by men and women who'd walked across America, and decided that while this sounded difficult, it was not impossible. So I started planning the journey, in my head at first.

My mother had died several years before, and my father, now in his mid-nineties, was ailing. He had dementia and was blind from glaucoma. I did not want to embark on a journey while he was alive, so I waited. My journey would either happen or not. Patience was called for.

But I kept planning. Still in my head. And one evening, I talked to my wife about it.

Sharon is a no-nonsense, practical, "show me the facts" type of person. She does not tolerate fools (we've been together over 35 years, so I wonder how and why she tolerates me, but that's another issue), and as a retired attorney as well as a person who likes to do taxes, she can analyze problems large and small.

So when I broached the subject, she asked for more information. I told her about the proposed trip, what I'd learned from reading, research, and study, and said I would not do this while my father was still alive.

Sharon never expressed doubt or tried to dissuade me (which shows you the kind of person she is and why I married her), so now it was up to me.

And the time was "now." At 70 years old I was not getting any younger.

Although there were people older than I who had successfully walked from coast-to-coast, each year that went by decreased my own chances of success. Thus, "now" was the time.

My father, Michael W. Schoen, passed away on March 7, 2017, at age 96.

After his funeral and dealing with his estate, I went ahead with my plans to walk from coast-to-coast. I decided to dedicate my journey to my father as a way to honor his life and his service as a World War II veteran who flew 44 missions as the flight

engineer and top turret gunner in a B-24 bomber in the Army Air Corps.

Five weeks later I was on the road. (That was my first mistake—I'd started too late in the year to avoid the extreme desert heat.)

Research and Google Maps pointed me to Huntington Beach, California, and the foot of the Santa Ana River Trail. This would be my starting point.

In the days preceding my departure I was totally occupied putting things together and running around to the Apple store, the Verizon store, the hardware store, the post office, and to grocery stores in an attempt to be as prepared as I could. My feelings of anticipation and angst were at a high level that would not end until I dipped my feet in the water and started my journey.

I rented a humongous white Toyota 4Runner and loaded it up with the Runabout kart I'd ordered from the designer at no small expense. Except for a few Easter Sunday fender-benders, the drive south from Oakland was smooth. Sharon and I checked into a motel and unloaded all our stuff. Then we drove to nearby John Wayne Airport, dropped off the rental car, and got a ride back to the motel.

The next morning, April 17, 2017, Sharon and I were joined by my longtime friend and optometry colleague, Dr. Bronson Hamada, who lives and practices in Huntington Beach.

I then waded into the Pacific Ocean and prepared to take the single step that would begin my longest journey.

Peach Springs, Arizona **Day 23**

My fingers were freezing, and my gloves, legs, and shoes were soaked. I'd been walking up and down hills in the rain for hours.

Earlier that morning I was stopped by the police. The two officers said they'd received reports that "a man pushing a stroller was walking on the wrong side of the road" (*untrue*) and "weaving in and out of the lane" (*true,* because there was no shoulder!).

As one officer called in my driver's license, I chatted with the other. When I came up clean we shook hands and they wished me a safe journey.

I arrived at the Hualapai Lodge in Peach Springs about 2 p.m. I was cold, wet, and hungry and didn't give a damn *what* the room cost—it was the only game in town. The desk clerk grudgingly admitted there was a room available, and then there was the business about my AARP card, which was "printed" vs. plastic.

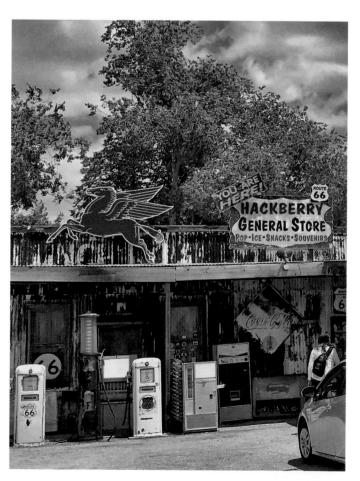

I ate lunch, hung up my wet stuff, and went for a soak in the Jacuzzi where I met Amanda and Troy, two nurses from Vail cycling across the country. Later we ate dinner together and shared two desserts.

Day 24　*Hualapai Reservation, Route 66, Arizona*

Ten minutes out of town the next morning, I encountered Officer Minoggio from the previous day waiting for me, hands on his hips and a smile on his face.

He greeted me warmly. "Our police report is on its way to Seligman, so if anyone gets a report of someone walking on the highway, they'll know it's probably you. Our report indicates you have 'sufficient means' and that you're walking in honor of your father." As we parted he added, "The eyes of Arizona are watching over you." Sounded good to me.

As I listened to Beethoven's *Symphony No. 3 (Eroica),* a crusty old guy in a Chevy 4X4 pulled up. A brown Labrador was riding shotgun. "Where the hell you going?" he asked. IIis cap read, "Don't Tread on Me," and he had a Colt .45 sitting on his dashboard. We chatted and he wished me luck.

Later I met Andy, a cyclist. I quickly diagnosed him as a misanthropic alarmist. He was convinced that I'd soon be killed by a tornado, cyclone, or baseball-sized hail stones. Beats a heart attack on the golf course.

Seligman, Arizona   **Day 25**

This morning, Officer Minoggio of the Hualapai Police stopped by once again to say hello. I was touched by his continued concern for me.

A couple of hours later I called Police Department headquarters and asked the woman who answered if I could speak to the police chief or leave him a message. She paused, then asked if I had a complaint. "No, just the opposite."

A few seconds later I heard, "This is Chief Bradley." When I introduced myself, the chief knew exactly who I was. I told him how I felt about Officers Goins and Minoggio—two good men who are sensitive and caring professionals in one of the toughest lines of work there is. Chief Francis E. Bradley, Sr., seemed pleased to get positive feedback about his officers and told me he'd be following my progress.

Seligman, a quaint tourist town on Old Route 66, seems to be doing better than many of the ghost towns created when I-40 displaced Route 66.

Day 26   *Ash Fork, Arizona*

Today was my first day walking on the Interstate.

But first I walked 18 miles on a beautiful stretch of Old Route 66 along gently rolling hills, with the sound of birds all around me. I listened to Jim Hall's recording of *Concierto de Aranjuez.*

Eventually I came to I-40 and was nervous. People, including an Arizona police officer, had assured me I could walk on the Interstate as long as I was wearing clothes and wasn't drunk.

Once on I-40 I met a cyclist. Florian Ohse had ridden from Chicago. He was a German living in Switzerland, and we chatted for a few minutes. I even dredged up a few German words (I studied German at Wantagh High School), and we became Facebook friends.

I walked the next seven miles on the noisy 8-foot-wide shoulder to the Flagstone Capital of the USA, Ash Fork, a town filled with empty storefronts and some charming but unoccupied houses.

I was back in the 1950s and my legs were stiff after walking 25 miles.

Williams, Arizona   Day 27

Today was uphill all day. Up, up, up, from Ash Fork to Willis, a long, slow climb of almost 18 miles, much of it against a headwind.

I don't know why some towns, like Williams, seem to have survived the Route 66 to I-40 transition better than others. It probably has to do with proximity to the new highway or other geographical and demographic factors.

Tonight I had a great meal at El Corral restaurant and got to speak some Spanish to the family that owns it.

Walking on the Interstate exposes you to a wide variety of road kill including owls, jack rabbits, a peccary, and today a large deer. Frankly, it's all sad and rather creepy.

Day 28   *Bellemont, Arizona*

"No, sir, it *is* illegal for pedestrians to walk on the Interstate. No matter what you were told." That's what the Arizona Highway Patrol officer informed me when he gave me the written warning. "And yes, cyclists *are* permitted." Feels like discrimination against us lonely pedestrians.

A half-mile later I exited the Interstate and began walking on the Old Route 66 frontage two-lane blacktop. It was fine until the pavement ended and I was walking on a dirt road.

Things got even worse when I saw a sign that said, "Entering Private Land."

As the wind and temperature fluctuated wildly by the minute, I walked on, a tough 23 miles today. If you think walking along "Old Historic Route 66" sounds charming, please revise your notion.

Flagstaff, Arizona **Days 29–30**

After the disappointment and difficulty of the previous day, I'd had enough of "Historic Route 66." After walking a few miles I accepted a ride into Flagstaff.

I checked into the Best Western Pony Soldier Inn and then I wandered down to Burger King for a fish sandwich, fries, and a Dr Pepper.

After lunch I sat in the Jacuzzi and pondered my situation.

Later I looked at routes out of Flagstaff. None looked promising.

I walked over to the Sportsman's Warehouse and tried on many shoes before buying a pair of Merrells. I offered Bailey, the salesgirl, advice on fitness, diet, and guys.

Across the street at Fat Olive's Wood Fired Pizzeria & Italian

Kitchen I ordered a pizza and the fire-roasted vegetable special. (I even ate the Brussels sprouts.)

I had to make a big decision. Soon.

Day 31   *Tempe, Arizona*

Sometimes you have to go south to go north.

How best to leave Flagstaff? Crazy climbs and altitude (north via Tuba City)? Miles of desert and scrub (Indian Reservations)? And what about the lack of services (water, food, lodging) and the inevitable dirt paths and interstate highways? I had to decide. How long could I hole up at the Best Western and sit in the Jacuzzi?

My sister's high school friend, Bruce Aiken, a respected artist living in Flagstaff, was not encouraging. He told me that walking north to Tuba City would include many miles of isolation.

Up to now I'd been following the route of Ben Davis, who encountered snow and the coldest days of his journey on his route from Flagstaff to Colorado.

When I called my friend Jeff Rudisill, he said, "Well, if you were in Phoenix, that's the way *I* went on my walk across the country."

I finally decided to reposition my walk 150 miles south to Phoenix. (I'll be walking those 150 miles later when I head north again.)

So I took a Greyhound bus to Phoenix and walked six miles to Tempe. There I met up with Lisa Monheit, an opera singer, speech pathologist, and 1973 graduate of Wantagh High School. We'd both benefitted from the mentorship of Rollan Masciarelli, a wonderfully talented and inspirational music teacher who changed our lives as musicians and people. "Maz" was that kind of teacher.

When Lisa asked what I needed, I said, "chocolate chip cookies." She didn't fail me!

Apache Junction, Arizona

Day 32

Today the world was flat, and most of the 25 miles I walked featured a paved sidewalk. But the day was not without drama.

After an early Egg McMuffin breakfast, I crossed paths with a guy towing a red trailer behind his bicycle. At first glance I thought he was a long-distance cyclist. But as he got closer he began ranting about somebody having stolen his f-ing backpack, and I realized he was a loco homeless guy with a lot of junk and a live puppy in his trailer. He became convinced that I'd stolen his backpack and yelled at me to open my kart.

I quickly determined my escape route and grabbed my can of bear spray. Then I yelled at *him*. "Move away and stop bothering me!"

He saw the can I was holding, turned his bike around, and rode away with the puppy and trailer. He never stopped ranting and cursing.

The guy had been scary, so I decided to call 911. Frankly, sometimes I don't know why I bother to do "the right thing." The dispatcher asked me if the guy was armed or if a crime had been committed. *No* and *No*. I realized that I was the only person who had been armed; I could also imagine a bad ending to this story. So I went on my way.

No good deed goes unpunished.

Day 33 US Route 60, Arizona

In my professional opinion, it is no safer to walk on State Highway 60 (I walked on it for 18 miles today) than on Interstate I-40, which I was kicked off of several days ago. This still annoys me.

Yes, there are differences having to do with exits and entrances, speed limits, gas stations and shopping centers, and noise levels. But I did not find one safer than the other when walking on the shoulder. Thanks for letting me rant.

I'm now in my tent, drinking water and Gatorade and sweating profusely. I've eaten two sandwiches (peanut butter and jelly, and American cheese and mustard), each heated courtesy of the sun. My drinks are cold courtesy of my 45° Latitude thermoses.

Today I passed sculptured images of Kokopelli, the flute-playing fertility deity, as well as ADA-compliant curb ramps that, like Tevye's staircases, go nowhere.

Don't you wish that your school was named *Superstition High School*? I do!

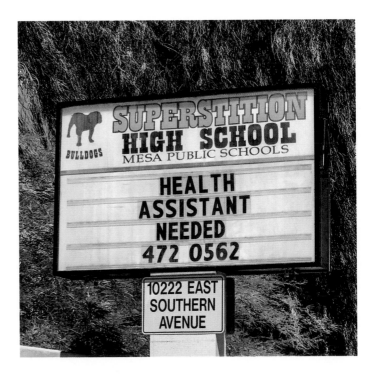

Superior, Arizona   Day 34

Sleeping in my tent is satisfying in a number of ways. There's plenty of room for me and my stuff and everything's within arm's reach. My air mattress is comfortable. I can see the stars through the mesh. And it generally costs nothing.

The downside is the desert heat until the sun sets. And of course there's no bathroom.

Amy at the Copper Mountain Motel in Superior put me in Room 4 ("Two beds, no extra charge").

Just beyond the town (pronounced "Sperior" by locals) is the Queen Creek Tunnel, built in 1952. It's 42 feet wide and 1,217 feet long, and I've been warned by everyone *not* to walk through it. Since I hear the mantra, *Be safe* every day, I'm getting a ride through the tunnel.

Day 35   *Globe, Arizona*

My 9 a.m. ride finally showed up at 10:30. She was smoking a cigarette and upset that she was going to lose her job.

Since I well know that most people have bigger problems than I do, I was empathetic as we drove through the narrow tunnel—impossible to walk through *with or without* the kart. And the winding road up to the town of Top-of-the-World was also scary, with no real shoulder, speeding vehicles, and many blind curves.

As I've said many times: *If this were easy, more people would do it.*

My driver calmed down as she told me about the "old" tunnel, the copper mines, and the karaoke bar.

After she dropped me in Miami and I gave her some much-appreciated cash, I walked seven miles in the heat to my motel at the far end of town, stopping at Safeway to buy fruit and kale salads, Wheat Thins, and some bananas.

San Carlos, Arizona   **Day 36**

I was out the door of the motel at 5 a.m. and out the door of McDonald's with my egg McMuffins 15 minutes later. A two-mile walk took me to the Hwy 70 entrance, and for many miles the shoulder was wide; until it wasn't.

I stopped for lunch at Apache Burger, where I asked, "Is there anything that's not meat or chicken? Like fish?"

"Sure. We have the fried shrimp combo." I settled on the kid's grilled cheese meal with fries. The kiddy-sized drink came in a plastic cup with a snap-on lid—perfect when camping for use during the middle of the night.

After a 25-mile day, I set up my tent behind some bushes off Hwy 70. Twenty-five miles is no longer impossible, but when you combine uphill climbs, a hot sun, and sore feet, it *is* a challenge.

It was still in the 90's at the end of the day, with absolutely *no* shade anywhere. But once the sun sets and the stars come out, my Kelty tent beats any motels I've stayed in.

Day 37   *Geronimo, Arizona*

Anyone who thinks walking across the country is about walking, I'm here to tell you that it's not.

Regardless, I managed to walk 25 miles again today. Starting at 5 a.m. tomorrow, I hope to do the same. It will be another 100°+ day.

In Bylas, I sat under a tree and rested while eating Skippy and Wheat Thins. Later I stopped at Mt. Turnbull Apache Market and enjoyed a Rocky Road ice cream cone and a Dr Pepper, filled my thermoses with water and ice, and received a "Be safe" from the staff.

Dorothea at the Public Health Department asked if I had water. I did. Her parting words? "Be safe!"

Later a Highway Patrol officer waved, and I waved back. No harm—I'm not on an Interstate highway.

At 4:15 p.m. my tent was set up amongst some tall bushes. No TV and little drama. Just heat, blisters, and a scratched leg from a surprise pop-up branch on the road. Immediate first aid applied.

Safford, Arizona   Day 38

Even though I'm in the best condition I've ever been, my third consecutive 25-mile walking day was the most grueling.

I was on the road at 4:40 a.m. Two hours later a guy in a pickup pulled up and handed me a plastic bag with two donuts in it. "I saw you yesterday—you must have walked 20 miles!"

"25, actually." He laughed and drove away.

I continued to see tons of roadside litter and had another run-in with a dog.

At Taylor Freeze I ate lunch. A couple of truckers recognized "my rig." "You're carrying a pistol, I'm sure. It's dangerous out there." I didn't want them to worry, so I just nodded. As they were leaving, one guy said, "Be safe!"

With an ice-water–soaked bandanna under my hat, I finally straggled into the Safford Best Western. I put my dirty clothes into the sink to soak and then soaked my brave feet in the pool. It's hot out there!

Day 39   *Solomon, Arizona*

Ants! Always when you least expect them!

After walking 15 miles in unbearable heat, I'd found a suitable site for my tent, set it up, and collapsed inside.

While waiting for the sun to set, I FaceTimed with Sharon. Looking over at my yellow squeeze bottle of mustard, I noticed it was completely covered with ants. They were the little black ones, marching from one end of my tent to the other. Their entrance was a *tiny* opening in a corner of the tent.

I dropped the phone and grabbed my roll of paper towels. I didn't have *Raid,* but I did have *Off!*

After obliterating the invading army and dragging the tent to a new location away from the nest, I sealed the entry hole with duct tape, crawled inside the tent, and collapsed.

Earlier in the day a pretty young woman in a small red car pulled over and asked, "Are you okay? Do you need a ride?"

I gave Georgianna a card and asked her, "Where were you planning to put my kart?"

She laughed. "I hadn't thought about that. I could give you some money, but I don't have much now. Maybe I can mail you some?"

"Thanks for the offer, but I'm okay, really."

She thought a moment. "How about prayers?"

"Perfect! I can *always* use some prayers!"

(Right now I'm praying for no more ants.)

Duncan, Arizona   **Day 40**

With temperatures heading into the 100's, it's time for me to admit defeat. I've walked through the cold and the rain, climbed up and down mountains, and endured pain. The heat almost killed me once in the Mojave Desert, and I can see and feel the results it is having on my body now. There's just no point in letting it finish the job.

I started my journey too late in the year; I didn't want to wait. I could have headed north from Flagstaff; had I done that I would have hit big snowstorms.

I was not aware that the high desert provided little shade for use in escaping from the heat. I've continued to lose weight in spite of drinking and eating all day long. And it's getting more difficult to keep my spirits and motivation up knowing I've still got so much more of the Southwest to walk through.

On a day like today I would have been willing to *pay* for shade!

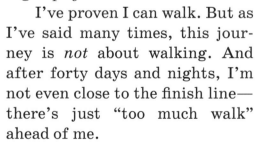

I've proven I can walk. But as I've said many times, this journey is *not* about walking. And after forty days and nights, I'm not even close to the finish line—there's just "too much walk" ahead of me.

I appreciate the tremendous support and encouragement from friends, relatives, and many strangers. But right now I don't feel the need to challenge Death. I'll leave that to others.

The Next Four Days

The Simpson Hotel, Duncan, Arizona

I called the Simpson Hotel/Bed & Breakfast in Duncan at 7:30 a.m. and Deborah, the owner, answered. I asked her, "If I were to arrive in an hour, would I be able to get breakfast?" She laughed. "Sure, we can make you some breakfast!"

I walked the eight miles into town, and frankly, it wasn't easy. I was running on fumes.

Arriving hungry and exhausted, I was welcomed by Deborah's husband, Clayton, who showed me to my room. I immediately fell in love with the old, restored hotel. I showered and sat down alone in a dining room filled with lovely antiques and paintings. True to her promise, I was served a *terrific* breakfast of multigrain griddle cakes made with hemp milk and topped with agave syrup, plus a roasted frittata with shallots, garlic, spinach, and cheddar cheese. The whole time I'm thinking, "I want to *live* here!"

After breakfast I rested. Sadly, I felt only failure and disappointment.

Because of a limited airline flight schedule and the Memorial Day holiday, I stayed on a few days. Two months would have been fine. I needed to rest, recover, and escape the stifling heat.

The Simpson Hotel is a six-room, 100-year-old restored property on one acre. It's been transformed with brick structures, a goat cave, pools, an organic garden, and an art studio, and it has a special vibe. Cats, goats, birds, and the neighbor's roosters and chickens provide plenty to observe and hear.

Three bikers who work for the Border

Patrol in Las Cruces stayed one night, and after breakfast I got to sit on George's Indian. Later Rudy took me for a short ride on his Harley.

Deborah and Clayton continued to treat me like family. They drove me to Stafford, where I shipped Walker home, while thunderstorms finally provided some relief from the heat.

The following morning I caught a Greyhound to Mesa and then a plane to Oakland. In spite of my feelings of disappointment and loss, I am aware of the many blessings I've received along the way.

I have a personal theory I call *The Half-life of Disappointment* that says: The deeper a disappointment, loss, or failure, the longer it takes to recover from it.

In time I'm sure I'll recover from my disappointment. No one was harmed, no one died, and the money I spent trickled down into the economy. I have memories that will last a lifetime, and I've met people with whom I developed special relationships.

Riding the bus past towns I'd recently walked through made it feel as if I were living the last few weeks of my life in reverse and in fast-motion. I still wake up at various hours of the night thinking, "I could have done it if …"

Yet some things are just not meant to be. I gave it my best shot, but I couldn't make it happen. That said, I certainly had an incredible adventure. Thanks to everyone who was with me on this journey. I am truly blessed.

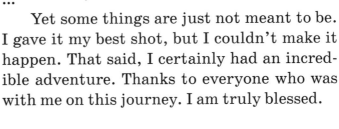

Failure and Disappointment

Experiencing failure is part of life. It's just a part we prefer to avoid.

After walking 40 days in parts of California and Arizona that I began to think of as *the Wilderness,* I approached the New Mexico border knowing I'd reached the limits of my endurance. The forecasts were the same each day—temperatures in the 90's and beyond. Heat and more heat. It was summer in the Southwest. People began to use the term "heat dome" to describe the situation.

Occasionally I reminded myself that had I headed north when I was in Flagstaff, I could have avoided all this heat. But then I remembered I would have instead walked straight into the snow. I guess I picked my poison.

Just a few weeks earlier, the intense heat of the Mojave Desert had almost killed me before I was rescued and escaped to Kingman. Now once again I could feel myself succumbing. Been there, done that.

Anyone familiar with the high desert knows there is rarely any shade under which to hide. In fact, the phrase "nowhere to hide" was on my mind all the time. I would have been happy to *pay* for shade!

In spite of drinking water all day I knew I was losing weight, and it was getting difficult to keep my spirits up and my motivation high. Winston Churchill once said, "Success consists of going from failure to failure without a loss of enthusiasm." Sorry, Winston, but I was losing my enthusiasm.

What was even sadder was that I'd already demonstrated that I could walk. Then again, I'd also come to realize that this journey was never about walking in spite of what people might imagine. And after only 40 days, there was still a lot of distance ahead of me.

The emotion I felt most was anger. After all, it was not my inability to walk 25 miles in a day, or push my kart up demanding hills, or negotiate ridiculous roads as trucks sped by at 75 mph—none of these challenges had defeated me. It was the heat— something totally out of my control.

The heat dome caused temperatures around Phoenix to reach as high as 119°. And that heat remained trapped in the area even after the sun went down. I'd walked 600 miles in 40 days. How long it would take me to recover from this major disappointment remained to be seen. But what I knew for sure was this experience was one of the greatest failures of my life, and the taste was bitter.

In the end, I decided not to challenge Death. I'd leave that to others. To survive, I'd have to abort my journey. I chose not to come home in a box.

Why Wouldn't You Want to Finish What You Started?

The misery of failure and pain of disappointment followed me home after my 40-day walk. I was welcomed home by family and friends, all expressing their relief that I'd returned safely. I did my best to put on a happy face, swallow my pride, and ignore the bitter taste of defeat. But I grieved, mostly in silence.

My "Half-life of Disappointment" theory ("The deeper a disappointment, loss, or failure is, the longer it takes to recover from it") proved to be true. As the months passed, my disappointment did slowly dissipate. I re-entered life, resumed my exercise reg-imen, returned to a normal diet, began playing piano with my jazz combo, and rejoined the flute section in the community concert band. I read, wrote, trav-eled, and eventually regained my physical and emo-tional health.

I'm not sure when the idea of resuming my jour-ney began; perhaps it never left.

When I broached the subject with my wife Sha-ron, she said, "Why *wouldn't* you want to finish what you started?"

My son, Adam, came to my rescue. We decided he would shadow me in a car for a few weeks as I made my way through the desert and beyond, dropping me off each morning and picking me up at the end of the day until I got to a point where I'd be able to avoid the Interstate highway system completely.

In late January 2018 I rented a car and drove to Palm Springs Airport where I met Adam's flight from Cin-cinnati (via Houston). We headed towards Needles, California, which would serve as our initial base of operations. I looked forward to spending time with my son on a road trip, something we hadn't done in many years.

On February 1, 2018, I was back on Route 66.

Sadly, in spite of walking in the same shoes that had previously been terrific, I began develop-ing blisters on my feet. After a hundred miles, I was through. My left foot was swollen, and I was advised at the urgent care center to start the antibiotic they prescribed and discontinue walking.

How many hits could I take? I dropped Adam at the Phoenix airport and then drove home. It was a long, lonely, depressing ride. Sharon was waiting up for me when I arrived. My mind was already process-ing a variety of plans.

The following morning I saw a podiatrist at

Kaiser. He told me the X-ray revealed no fracture and that I should just rest my foot. I got the impression he was used to dealing with a wide variety of sports-related injuries, and this was not one of the really serious ones. He predicted things would get better soon, and they did. I mostly stayed at home as my foot healed, and worked out the logistics of resuming my journey.

Two weeks later, my kart, my perfectly healed left foot, and I were aboard a Greyhound bus headed to Las Cruces, New Mexico. The next morning was Day 47 on the road.

I continued to walk another 1,900 miles through 12 more states. It was 123 more days through cold, heat, wind, and rain. I walked up and down thousands of feet of elevation as I endured bedbugs, flies, bad motels, and poor roads until I finally reached the Atlantic. Along the way I visited my children, their spouses, and my grandsons; high school and college classmates; old friends and new

friends; and I met angels who were kind, caring, and generous.

Anyone who has read my blog posts or has done any hiking at all understands that this journey was no simple task. It required strategic planning and careful use of resources, both material and financial.

I've been asked, "What kept you going?" Here's one answer I can give: It's in my nature to complete things I start. I can actually trace this desire for closure to an experience I had in high school. I was a Boy Scout on track to become an Eagle Scout. This required attaining 21 merit badges. I had 17, including most of the "difficult" ones, when I became distracted by girls and rock 'n' roll. I didn't realize how important this goal was to me until I was over the age limit (18) to qualify. I came so close. I believe the experience of not completing a desired task that I was capable of achieving was an important life lesson for me.

I still laugh when I recall that I was only one class away from getting my associate degree from Laney College when I was accepted to the University of California Berkeley School of Optometry. (This was my purpose in attending Laney in the first place.) Four years later I received a doctorate from Cal, but I never forgot about that associate degree. Ten years later I enrolled in and completed a Spanish class at Laney, applied for the degree, and received my diploma.

So it was no shock to me that even though it took me three attempts, I persevered until I finally waded into the Atlantic Ocean. As I said, closure is in my nature. And the fact that I didn't succeed the first or even second time made achieving my goal even sweeter.

Chambless, California   **Day 41**

Poof! ...It is February 1, and I'm back on Route 66.

After walking 600 miles last spring in an attempt to walk coast-to-coast, I discontinued my journey as temperatures in parts of the southwest reached 119°. I do not have a Death Wish and so decided to live to walk another day. That "other day" is today.

When he heard that I planned to resume my walk, my son, Adam, asked if he could be of assistance. I gratefully accepted his help. For the next few weeks Adam would drop me off in the morning and pick me up in the afternoon. We'd also get to spend some time together. While I make up the 100 miles I didn't walk last spring due to the "heat dome," we're staying in Needles for a few nights.

Today I walked 18 miles. My back is sore and my feet hurt. Otherwise, it feels great to resume my journey.

Day 42

Goffs Road, Old Route 66, California

Adam dropped me off early, and I had an uneventful walk on Old Route 66. Although the area I'm walking on is closed to general traffic, I saw many construction trucks, and all of the drivers returned my wave.

As I got closer to I-40, the road started to parallel the railroad tracks, and for the rest of the day freight trains going in both directions passed by. On one train I counted 200 cars. Several engineers waved.

Around lunchtime I started dragging, and to pick myself up I began to whistle the Colonel Bogie March. But whistling takes energy, so I quit. Instead I listened to the album, "The Greatest Marches of John Philip Sousa." Sousa is a hero of mine. He was one of the most celebrated (and wealthiest) composers and band leaders of his time, and his music helped me pick up my pace considerably.

At Najah's Oasis rest stop (a tacky, overpriced Route 66 joint run by bored teenagers) I bought a root beer and a Snickers, sat at an outside table, and ate a can of Progresso Chicken Noodle Soup.

Because of a painful blister on the sole of my left foot, the last five miles were difficult.

After lunch, I listened to Beethoven's *Symphony No. 1*. I think Ludwig would have liked Sousa.

Goffs, California

Day 43

Not much in the town of Goffs in spite of the population listed on the sign. I saw no one, not even a mouse.

At a railroad crossing I chatted with a guy as a freight train passed. He and his wife were on their way to Laughlin. "So am I," I said. He wished me "Good luck," and she told me, "Be safe."

The blister on my left foot seemed to be getting worse and my back wasn't happy either. So I tried "the best medicine" after laughter and drugs—music.

First was "Entrance of the Gladiators" by Julius Fučík (1897), which will cheer anybody up!

Next up was *Time Out* by the Dave Brubeck Quartet (1959). I

know every note of that LP, including the drum solos. Then *Abbey Road* (1969), which coincided with my move from Boston to San Francisco.

During 16 miles of walking today there was not a drop of shade anywhere.

Day 44

Dead Mountains Wilderness Area, Arizona

I walked into a light headwind all day. The temperature was pleasant.

At one point a freight train loaded with tanks and jeeps passed by, and soon I turned onto Route 95, ending my pleasant albeit lonely walk on Route 66.

Route 95 was pretty much hell to walk on. Constant trucks and cars headed my way forced me on and off the narrow sand and gravel shoulder and required extreme vigilance.

I passed Camp Ibis where in 1942 General George S. Patton, Jr., located a "North Africa–like desert training site."

Dead Mountains Wilderness Area was where I stopped to eat my lunch. I was joined by a large number of ants, which always seem to find me.

I'm heading toward Laughlin, which will be our new HQ for the next few nights. By the time Adam picked me up, my feet (and the rest of me) were exhausted.

Bullhead City, Arizona   Day 45

Sidewalks!

After walking 10 miles on packed dirt roads and narrow shoulders I entered Bullhead, Arizona, and walked on real sidewalks for another 10 miles.

Highway 95 is a city road, featuring constant traffic and many shops and services. Some of the billboards and signage made me laugh. I particularly liked the law firm of "Lerner & Rowe," as well as the poor cat who's pregnant yet again.

Jerome Kern is the featured Composer of the Day, and one of my favorites. It was through him that I learned how to incorporate different tonal centers when composing a song—"All the Things You Are" is the perfect example.

I listened to his greatest hits for over an hour.

As I soaked my feet in the hotel's Jacuzzi, Adam worked from our room. He's very good at what he does, and his business continues to grow. It's been a pleasure having him with me.

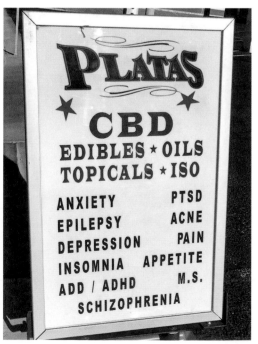

Day 46
and Another Trip Home

State Route 68, Arizona

Today's walk took me from Bullhead City, past Laughlin, and toward Kingman.

The road just climbed and climbed until I reached Union Pass at 3,571' and gazed at the city of Kingman as it appeared in the valley below. I was fighting a mild headwind the entire day, but the paved shoulder was wide.

I listened to *Symphony in C,* which Georges Bizet wrote as a student at age 17; it was never performed in his lifetime. Later the Beatles *Revolver* album (1966) brought back many memories.

Mesa, Arizona

Sadly, music has not been enough to cure my physical maladies. A large blister on my left foot finally broke and the foot is red and painful. I became depressed knowing it would take time to heal. I'd just walked 17 miles.

With increasing pain and swelling of my left foot and toes

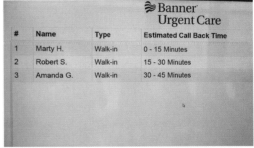

#	Name	Type	Estimated Call Back Time
1	Marty H.	Walk-in	0 - 15 Minutes
2	Robert S.	Walk-in	15 - 30 Minutes
3	Amanda G.	Walk-in	30 - 45 Minutes

Banner Urgent Care

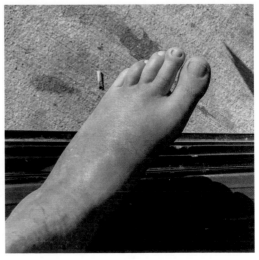

I visited an urgent care facility in Mesa, where I was prescribed an antibiotic and told to rest the foot. I'd been doing well, but without healthy feet, there's no walk.

For the second time—and after walking over 700 miles in total—I'd had to give up my long-desired wish to walk across the USA. Needless to say, it was a sad and disappointing day for me.

After a sleepless night I went online at 5:30 a.m. and booked a flight home for Adam. It was his birthday the following day and I wanted him to be able to spend it with his wife and son.

We checked out of the hotel and drove to the Phoenix airport, where Adam and I said goodbye. Then I began the long drive home to Oakland. I had an appointment set up with the Kaiser podiatrist the following morning.

Oakland, California

When I arrived home many hours later, Sharon was waiting up for me. I ate some real food, had a few words with the cat, and went to bed. As I fell asleep, I thought about the lesson I'd learned time and again: Walking across the country is *not* about walking.

Day 47 — *Oakland, California to Las Cruces, New Mexico*

The podiatrist who examined my foot told me the X-ray revealed no fractures and that I just needed to rest it. Two weeks later, after testing it on a few three-mile hikes, I was ready to resume my journey.

I once again said goodbye to Sharon and Graciela (wife and cat, respectively), and walked from our Lake Merritt home to the Downtown Oakland Greyhound bus terminal.

Twenty-eight hours later I arrived in Las Cruces, New Mexico, where I would begin the next stage of my long journey. (I chose Las Cruces because it was close to where I'd terminated my walk in 2017. It would also allow me to avoid walking on the Interstate.)

A Lyft SUV took me from the so-called bus station (a convenience store) to the Best Western, where I re-bolted the container holding all my stuff to Walker, my trusty kart.

In the morning I ate the complimentary breakfast, purloined a few hard boiled eggs for the road, bought three gallons of water at Dollar General and a tuna sub at Subway, and then took my sweet time walking 17 miles on the Bataan Memorial Highway to Organ, New Mexico. (My feet did fine.)

At the Patti Ann Mobile Trailer Park, Weston, the owner, graciously allowed me to pitch my tent for the night, gratis. Another angel helping me along my journey.

Highway 70, New Mexico

Day 48

It was quiet at the Patti Ann when I departed. The night had been windy and cold. I slept in my long underwear, two pairs of wool socks, a wool shirt, and a wool cap. My sleeping bag is rated down to 19°F, but it was still *cold*.

It took me three hours to walk the first six miles, uphill and arduous. Then downhill for three more hours, as I fought Walker all the way, my right hand cramping from squeezing the handbrake. The sun was bright, but I wore my Patagonia jacket all day. By the time we finally hit level ground my feet and I were both tired.

After walking 15 miles, I camped behind a few scrawny bushes. At 6 p.m. the wind was picking up and it was getting colder. I texted my son, Adam, thanking him once more for helping in the des-

ert. Although our time together was cut short by blisters, he said once again, "It is what it is, Dad." Amen to that.

Day 49

*White Sands,
New Mexico*

No place to camp. The same old story.

I remind friends that this is not a sightseeing trip—no visits to national parks or monuments. But as my photos confirm, I see plenty. I'm getting a street-level view of the country. Some of it is beautiful and some is ugly. Most of the ugly comes from trash on the sides of the roads. The beauty comes from nature, courtesy of the Almighty.

The Artist of the Day is Kenny Burrell, a jazz guitarist from Detroit. I have his 1956 debut album on vinyl and saw him in 1965 when I was at Boston University. There was a time in my life when I thought I could play guitar. But it turns out to be one of the easiest instruments to play badly.

After walking 19 miles, I wasn't asking for much. Just a little privacy or protection from the wind on *this* side of the ubiquitous barbed wire.

A bird just started chirping nearby, hopefully a good omen.

Alamogordo, New Mexico

Day 50

Last night was cold and today was even colder. I was happy it wasn't raining. Or snowing.

Q: What do these songs have in common? Something Stupid; Hey Girl, I Heard You're Getting Married; Sittin' in La La (Waitin' For My Ya Ya); White Bird; The Boy From New York City; Girl, You'll Be a Woman Soon.

A: They are all part of the IHOP playlist I heard at dinner.

The mushroom and spinach omelet delivered by Cassie (a senior in high school) was fine; the pancakes were pancakes, and the salad was a large handful of Costco-type spring mix with cut up tomato. (As a Motel 6 guest, I got 10% off. Woo-hoo!)

Do you have a yen for sand dunes and missile ranges? Visit White Sands National Monument, where you can supposedly slide down the snow-like dunes on saucer sleds. Which I didn't.

Album of the Day: *Blue Train* by John Coltrane, a seminal recording. I also listened to more Sousa marches—they get the walking juices flowing. This is probably the first time Coltrane and Sousa showed up in the same paragraph.

Day 51   *Tularosa, New Mexico*

The elevation is increasing each day. Tularosa is at 4,508'.

The highway was under construction, but that was good news for me. Two lanes were blocked off by cones, and that's where I walked for two hours.

The motel I'd planned to stay in was "iffy," and as I sat thinking on my camp stool in front of a nice home on 2nd Street, the friendly homeowner came out to find out what I was up to. He invited me to stay in their home's workshop, and I accepted.

Jerry and his partner Ed join a growing list of angels along my journey.

Artist of the Day: Eddie Daniels, jazz and classical clarinetist and saxophonist extraordinaire, and a New Mexico resident.

I'll be in the tent on Hwy 54 for the next two cold, cold nights.

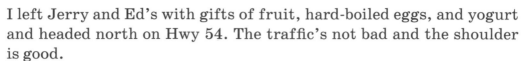

Highway 54, New Mexico

Day 52

I left Jerry and Ed's with gifts of fruit, hard-boiled eggs, and yogurt and headed north on Hwy 54. The traffic's not bad and the shoulder is good.

When there are no services on the road, meals can be a challenge. But today I had a great breakfast: blueberry yogurt with peanuts, raisins, almonds, dried apricots, and Triscuits. For lunch: hard-boiled

egg, Swiss cheese, more Triscuits, pistachio nuts, and chocolate covered Hostess mini-donuts (I *love* 'em!). Dinner was a two-serving can of Progresso Classic Chicken Noodle Soup (spooned straight from the can), an apple, more Triscuits, and a few more donuts. I drank water all day.

Album of the Day: *The Legendary João Gilberto: The Original Bossa Nova Recordings* (1958–1961). While his wife, Astrud, became famous in the US as a result of her recording in English of "The Girl From Ipanema," he was the real talent.

Once the sun sets out here, it gets cold fast. So, time to burrow into the Kelty!

Day 53

Highway 54,
New Mexico

Today began with an overcast, gray, gloomy sky. But by 1 p.m. the sun had come out and with it the wind, pushing me from behind. I just walked, took breaks, and listened to music and old *Fresh Air* interviews.

Whatever drivers of cars may think about truckers, I find most truck drivers to be courteous, observant, and professional. Often they go out of their way or change lanes to avoid driving too close to me. I first learned about the Doppler Effect in physics class at Laney College (look it up if you've never heard of it). Whether the truckers understand the underlying principal or not, I appreciate their efforts. When I wave, they pretty much always respond in kind.

Album/Composer of the Day: *Leroy Anderson's Greatest Hits.* Anderson was a Harvard educated Ph.D. He composed many songs and concert pieces, which he called "miniatures." I loved his music as a boy and still marvel at his orchestrations.

Carrizozo, New Mexico   **Day 54**

At 9:35 a.m. I saw flashing lights up ahead, but it turned out to be a surveying crew. I chatted with two of the guys, and they wished me luck.

On my way into Carrizozo, I stopped at the Dollar General for supplies, including lip balm—it's really dry at this elevation.

When Jubin, the owner of the Four Winds Motel, heard that I was walking in honor of my Dad, he insisted on giving me the veteran's discount. My room is clean and comfortable.

Album of the Day: *Gerry Wiggins Live at Maybeck Recital Hall.* I love how Wig plays, with sensitivity, richness, and humor. He worked

with everyone from Stepin Fetchit to Louis Armstrong to Lena Horn. This album is solo jazz piano at its finest.

It started raining this afternoon, and later hailed. Glad I'm inside tonight!

Day 55

Highway 54, New Mexico

Because the road this morning was slick after the rain, hail, and cold temperatures last night, I waited a while before hitting the road. At a local café I ate an overpriced, mediocre omelet and toast and ordered a couple of hard boiled eggs ($2 each) to go. The waitress called me "Honey" at least a dozen times.

The bright sun melted the frost along the road. It was a great day for walking as I headed toward Corona, elevation 6,690'. After 19 miles I finally set up my tent behind some actual evergreen trees.

Artist/Album of the Day: *Buddy Collette, Man of Many Parts.* This 1956 LP features Buddy on clarinet, sax, and flute. A childhood friend of Charles Mingus and a founding member of the Chico Hamilton Quintet, he enjoyed a long career as a performer, studio musician, and college instructor.

At 6 p.m. the temperature dropped quickly, along with the sun.

Corona, New Mexico

Days 56–57

The temperature dropped to 27° last night, and the cold seeped through my tent, air mattress, and sleeping bag.

And 27 also happens to be the number of miles I walked today—the most miles I've *ever* walked in a day. (I awoke rested in the morning. If you have difficulty sleeping at night, try walking 27 miles during the day.)

Tonight is Friday night, the beginning of Shabbat (the Sabbath), a traditional day of rest. Outside, a freight train rumbles by 50 yards from my motel window. I often hear the sound of trains in my dreams.

At the Corona Motel each room has a *theme*: Jungle; Bikers; Hollywood; Beach; etc. I chose the *1950s* room—I love it! On Saturday evening I joined the motel owners, Rhonda and George, and their friends Nancy and Eric for a drink (Dr Pepper for me). I learned that Corona (*crown*) is the highest point of the region, there are only 70 students in the entire school system, the kids only go to school Monday through Thursday because they're needed on the farms and ranches, showing their livestock at the State Fair is an excused school absence, and they only field basketball and track teams-—not enough kids for baseball or football. A different life.

Day 58   *Duran, New Mexico*

This morning was windy and a tailwind pushed me downhill from Corona. I'm now headed toward the Midwest.

Near the end of my 20-mile walk today, I passed Duran, pop. 35. It's basically a ghost town near the railroad track, a common story having to do with the evolution of the railroad industry, mining, and ranching.

A mile or two past Duran I spied a small trail through an open gate that led me to the best stealth camping site I've had since starting this journey. About time! I'm between Highway 54 and the railroad track, but surrounded by trees. I'm less exposed than usual.

Tomorrow I once again have no idea where I'll be sleeping. I'd say this feeling is the greatest source of stress I feel on my journey.

Vaughn, New Mexico   Day 59

Each evening at sundown, the temperature sinks quickly and the winds pick up.

I was awakened at 2:30 a.m. by the sounds of industrial machinery coming from the nearby railroad tracks. The noise lasted for two hours.

At 6 a.m. it was 27°, and when I stuck my head outside the tent the wind hit me like an icicle.

Due to major railroad repair going on in town, all the motel rooms were booked. Out of desperation I called an RV park and asked the woman if I could pitch my tent there. She said, "Call my brother Reuben. He might be able to help." And he did! Reuben owns the Bel-Air Motel and he saved a room for me.

Vaughn (pop. 446) seems in a sorry state. Built to serve the railroad, there was once a Harvey House in town, but it's not there now. (Neither is Judy Garland.)

Artist of the Day: What I love most about David Sedaris is that he reminds me of the last hour I spent with my sister-in-law, Gail Cohen, as she was dying of cancer. Usually her Kaiser hospital room was filled with women friends singing to her, holding her hands, and massaging her feet. But now she was alone and asked if I'd read to her. I picked up a Sedaris book that was on the table, and we spent an hour laughing together. That experience led me to an 8-year stint as a Kaiser volunteer.

Day 60

Highway 60, New Mexico

The day started in a railroad town motel and ended in a cow pasture.

Highway 60 is a two-lane blacktop with a narrow shoulder and sparse traffic. Police and sheriff's cars occasionally passed by and would respond to my wave, but they otherwise ignored me.

Although I did not see one tree or bush to hide behind, I finally spied an open pasture gate. I didn't see any cows, so I decided to go for it and set up my tent.

Later as I fell asleep, I thought, *If I hear even one moo, I'll start to worry.*

At 10 p.m. I awoke to the sounds of mooing! But it was cold and I wasn't budging. Through the tent's mesh roof I saw the Big Dipper directly above me. As I watched blinking satellites pass by, I was awed by the vastness of it all.

Highway 60, New Mexico

Day 61

Twenty-seven degrees keeps following me around. Today was pretty much gloomy and overcast, preceded by some wicked cold this morning.

Tonight I put the rain fly on my tent for the first time, hoping it will help. I'm camped in a public picnic area, so I'm not happy about not being able to see out.

I told Sharon that if the sheriff or police hassle me, I'll tell them to arrest me—there's just no place to camp on this long stretch of highway, and it's too cold to move.

My weather apps are predicting continued cold temperatures and rain over the next few days. I'm as prepared as I can be, but I am *so* looking forward to March going out like a lamb!

Day 62

Yeso, New Mexico

Yesterday I was introduced to *Tribulus terrestris*, more commonly known as Goathead weed or Puncturevine. It's one of the banes of the Southwest desert and a serious hazard to bare feet and bicycle tires. Even though the Internet says the plant is used medicinally for UTIs and to boost testosterone, these are *miserable* little devils. Cyclists hate them.

This morning the road was flatter and the weather quite pleasant as I passed through Yeso, a semi–ghost town filled with crumbling ruins—another railroad town that pretty much disappeared.

My fountain pen correspondent and friend, Skip, drove out from Santa Fe so we could spend some time together. He's a smart, funny guy, a great photographer, and a retired professor of psychology and statistics at Gallaudet University in D.C. We've corresponded for years, but never met. It's one of the interesting things about meeting a correspondent— you know each other, but you don't!

Fort Sumner, New Mexico

Day 63

When I think "Continental Breakfast," I picture Fred Astaire and Ginger Rogers sitting in evening clothes eating soft boiled eggs from little silver egg cups. Not so with the Super 8 Motel continental breakfast.

Skip dropped me where he'd picked me up the previous day, about 14 miles from the motel. As he drove toward Santa Fe, I walked back to Fort Sumner.

Sadly, I'm nursing a blister on my left foot yet again. I'm keeping it taped and wearing two pairs of socks.

When I reached town I ordered a fish sandwich, iceberg lettuce salad, and Mug root beer at Dariland [*sic*]. Then I spent the afternoon doing laundry, which includes everything I have with me (other than the shorts and T-shirt I was wearing).

Billy the Kid was shot in Fort Sumner (pop. approx. 1,000) by Pat Garrett and is buried in town. Later Garrett himself was shot and killed elsewhere "under unclear circumstances." *Live by the sword …*

Day 64   *Tolar, New Mexico*

When you make plans, sometimes life gets in the way. Sometimes death.

About 4 p.m. three sheriffs cars sped by, sirens blaring and lights flashing. Soon ambulances and a fire truck followed.

As I neared the scene of the accident, I saw a Broderick Crawford look-alike in a sheriff's uniform turning all vehicles away.

When he saw me, Crawford pointed to the road ahead and said, *"Do not* try walking past that!"

"I won't," I said and pointed to a nearby abandoned property. "I'm just going to stay up there."

"Okay," he said. In my mind, his reply constituted *tacit approval.*

I pushed Walker up the driveway, picked a suitable spot away from the Goathead weeds, and pitched my tent. Two hours later, the flashing police lights disappeared, but it was too late to continue walking.

Today was the anniversary of my father's death, and I said Kaddish for my dad.

It was really windy all night. Tomorrow is supposed to be colder with a 50% chance of morning rain.

Melrose, New Mexico   **Day 65**

If I hadn't been in my tent last night weighing it down, it would have blown into the next county.

Today the weather apps kept reporting rain "within 120 minutes," but so far, nothing.

It was cold and I walked at a brisk pace all day. When I passed the scene of yesterday's traffic accident I saw plenty of skid marks and car parts. No reports of fatalities. Yet.

I stopped for lunch at All-sup's (a chain of 300 convenience stores in New Mexico, Texas, and Oklahoma), and Shaun said hello. He'd seen me walking and wanted to know my story. Most people are just plain friendly.

After 23 miles I camped next to the railroad tracks. The freight trains may be noisy, but here there's less exposure to the highway.

Artist of the Day: Steve Martin, a very funny guy! I recommend his memoir, *Born Standing Up*.

When I called to make a motel reservation, the woman from Wyndham hotel group asked, "How may I grant your wish?"

Day 66   *Clovis, New Mexico*

The 7 a.m. freight train was my alarm clock this morning.

The road to Clovis was one continuous highway construction project. By noon the sun was out and the temperature was perfect for walking. Passing Cannon Air Force Base, I watched prop driven planes fly by overhead and walked past several good places where I could rent automatic weapons and buy ammo.

I ate lunch at Subway and then just kept walking. Hours later, I checked into Days Inn. The manager, Dharmesh, was friendly and curious about my journey. Later he invited me to join him, his wife Shilpa, and his two kids (Aahana and Aarav) for pizza. We talked about their home in India and their life in Clovis, their dreams for their kids, the American diet, gangs, and my walk. Pizza is often a common denominator.

Bovina, Texas   Day 67

Seven miles after leaving Clovis, I walked into Texas, my fourth state on the journey.

Texico (that's how you spell it) is the border town between the two states, a portmanteau of Texas and New Mexico. The things one learns on the road.

I had to deal with a barking dog who followed me down the highway. Personally I believe that mad dogs are a bigger threat to me than mad humans.

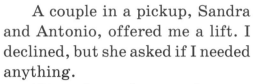

A couple in a pickup, Sandra and Antonio, offered me a lift. I declined, but she asked if I needed anything.

"Yes, I need someplace to pitch my tent tonight." Antonio asked where I was headed.

Two hours later I set up my tent beside their home in Bovina, where I met and chatted with their 17-year-old son, Antonio, Jr. When I told him that his mother was an angel, he agreed.

Later we all shared a meal and they invited me to stay in their spare bedroom. I'm blessed.

Day 68

Friona, Texas

I shed layers of clothing as the clouds parted and the sun warmed the day. As I walked along fields of farmland and grazing animals, there was not a tree in sight. Freight trains ran back and forth all day long, their whistles blowing at regular intervals.

In Friona, the Cheeseburger Capital of Texas, I ordered a fish sandwich at the Dairy Queen, but was told, "We don't have that no more."

So I walked across the street to Dollar General and bought a loaf of bread, a package of Swiss cheese, and a Dr Pepper. In my room I opened a packet of StarKist and enjoyed open-faced tuna and cheese sandwiches with mustard, heated in the microwave. Hostess Donettes for dessert completed the feast.

Tomorrow's temperatures are predicted to range from 42° to 77°. It's warming up!

Hereford, Texas   **Day 69**

On this *Ides of March* in 2018, I entered Deaf Smith County.

The name rang a bell for me—my sister and I remember my mother having Deaf Smith Peanut Butter in our house when we were kids. Erastus "Deaf" Smith (1787–1837) was an American frontiersman, soldier, and spy during the Texas Revolution. Although he didn't die at the Alamo, he was there for a while and later worked with General Sam Houston and the Texas Rangers. In the movie *The Alamo,* he was portrayed by teen idol Frankie Avalon.

The Hereford, Texas founder of Arrowhead Mills Co., named the peanut butter brand after Smith.

Today was "road kill" day. I saw a wide variety of species, including deer, raccoons, jackrabbits, skunks, barn owls and smaller birds, a fox, dogs, cats, and a rat.

Podcast of the Day: *Planet Money.* Both entertaining and informative.

Day 70   *Umbarger, Texas*

I had a visit from a BNSF Railway Company Police Department Senior Special Agent. Rick asked if I was "traveling through." I gave him my card and assured him I was. As he pulled away he told me to "Be safe."

While walking, the wind was at my back, the highway shoulders were generally wide, and there weren't any hills to speak of. The elevation of Amarillo is 3,605'. Compare this to Corona, NM, which was 6,690'.

Today I walked half the distance to Amarillo and pitched my tent next to the ever-present barbed wire fence. I've entered the Central time zone and am now on Daylight Saving Time.

Shabbat Shalom.

[I'd like to mention that virtually every photo taken on my journey that features the sun was taken at *sunrise—not* sunset. Remember: I'm heading East.]

Amarillo, Texas   Day 71

Other than the sound of freight train whistles, my night was comfortable and no one bothered me.

I was up before the sun, and while the temperature is no longer in the low 30's, it's still pretty chilly.

During my long walk on a stretch of VFW Rd., a Randall County sheriff told me to "Be careful."

A shortcut through The Colonies, a housing development with large cookie-cutter homes (many of which are for sale in the $500k range), afforded me some quiet time away from the highway.

I stopped at a Burger King, where the enthusiastic staff wished me, "Good luck!" and "Be safe!"

Day 72

Amarillo, Texas

Instead of spending the whole day in a motel room resting and going nuts, I decided I'd walk from one end of Amarillo to the other, a short, easy 12-mile day.

The first three miles was along Rock Island Rail Trail, one of many such trails that have been reclaimed from unused railroad routes and converted to walking/biking trails. Unfortunately the end of the trail dumped me in a pretty seedy part of Amarillo. So I moved a couple of blocks over. This had me walking along the busy I-40 access road, which featured a lot of traffic and no discernible shoulder. So I moved yet again onto a parallel street that took me through a few miles of modest Latino family neighborhoods and then back onto the noisy access road. Finally I spied my motel.

So much for a short, easy 12-mile day.

Panhandle, Texas   Day 73

A High Wind Advisory was in effect all night, with 30 mph winds and gusts much higher. When I attempted to go out for dinner, the wind was blowing so hard I just went back to my room. The desk clerk told me that wildfires threatened many nearby areas.

Since I did not want to spend a third night in Amarillo, at 10 a.m. I braved the wicked winds and headed out. The first few miles along the access road were rough going, but it was better once I hit Highway 60 itself. The strong headwind was a challenge all day, and setting up my tent was something out of Laurel and Hardy.

Tonight the winds are supposed to die down, but the temperature will be dropping into the 30's. I'm camped on a dirt road next to the barbed wire. Sadly, I'm also near a freight train crossing, so I'll be hearing train whistles all night.

Day 74   *White Deer, Texas*

I brushed some frost from my tent as I packed up my stuff on this first day of spring. It was 30°.

This is the way I look at it: "I've taken a job, and that job is to walk seven to nine hours a day." And frankly, I've had worse jobs (that summer working at the Hunt's cannery in Hayward comes to mind).

After an uneventful day of walking, I set up my tent on a county road next to the barbed wire. A friendly guy in a pickup pulled up. "Are you okay?" asked Ed, who farms wheat on the adjacent field. "Welcome to County Road X—'X marks the spot!'" We spoke for a few minutes about our parents and aging. Then he waved good-bye and said, "Be safe!"

Pampa, Texas   Days 75–76

The next morning, I walked a couple of miles to an Allsup's and chatted with Jackie while Sherry made me two egg and cheese breakfast sandwiches on croissants. They're as good as the Egg McMuffins at McDonald's and a third the price (hold the Canadian bacon, please).

Some of the roads I've been walking on are so narrow and winding that I have to move over to the other side of the road and walk *with* traffic. I normally don't do this, but everyone keeps telling me to "Be safe," so I am.

Artist of the Day: Scott Hamilton—the tenor saxophonist, not the skater. I've been a fan for decades. Scott's tone and intonation are beautiful, and whether the song is fast or slow, he plays with a beautiful, lyrical style. In addition, he plays all of my favorite songs.

My body and psyche needed a day of rest as I decided which direction to head next, so I stayed an extra day in Pampa. For help I turned once

again to Jeff Rudisill, who walked across the US several years ago.

Jeff is a Southerner, with an easy grace in his smiling voice. He puts me at ease in a moment, calms my fears, and assures me that all is well. I felt much better after our talk. The plan is to continue on Hwy 60 into Missouri.

I can honestly say that the mint chocolate chip ice cream cone from Braum's this afternoon was the best I've ever had in my life! For dinner, I enjoyed salmon on angel hair pasta, followed by a piece of chocolate cheesecake.

Pampa is Woody Guthrie country, and the song immortalized on the public sculpture is "This Land is your Land."

Miami, Texas

Day 77

Leaving Pampa this morning, I was sad to see many closed shops, garages, and restaurants, and long-abandoned homes and trailers.

I found a gun on the side of the road. After taking a photo of it, I wiped off my prints and put it back on the roadside.

Two days ago it was 30°, but tonight it was 94°. I'd camped in a cattle pasture off the road, and strong winds were buffeting my tent.

Shortly after I'd eaten, a man about my age pulled up in his pickup truck and said, "You shouldn't be here."

I asked politely if it would be okay if I stayed overnight. "I'll be out by 7 a.m."

"No, you don't understand. You shouldn't be *here!*" He pointed behind him, and it was then I saw the wildfires that were heading our way. The winds were high and gusting, and the distant clouds of smoke were thick.

David Locke, a fourth generation rancher, offered to take me seven miles up the road to the town of Miami where he felt I'd be safer. "There's no motel, though."

As the clouds of dark gray smoke got closer, we lifted my kart into his truck and drove to the town park where I set up next to a picnic table.

There were a lot of little kids playing in the park, but no one paid any attention to me.

David called back later to check on me. Another angel comes to my aid. Incredible.

Day 78

Canadian, Texas

It was quiet in the park until 4:30 a.m. when a dog in a nearby house started barking every 20-30 seconds. I got little sleep, but I'd dodged the wildfires. It was still dark when I started walking.

In the semi-darkness, I thought I heard the sound of horses' hooves! And indeed, six horses were galloping along behind the barbed wire beside me. It was quite thrilling to see and hear them.

I walked up and down hills for a few hours until I reached a rise and saw the plains stretched out before me. It was a magnificent view!

Around noon, I sensed movement near my leg and looked down to see two friendly dogs walking quietly beside me. They followed me for a mile or so, often wandering onto the highway as trucks whizzed by at 75 mph.

I'm getting close to Oklahoma.

Glazier, Texas   Day 79

"Hey, is that your dog?" a man asked as I walked by. He was doing yard work in front of his house. I turned around and saw the dog.

"No, it isn't." The dog and I looked at each other. I sighed and continued down the road.

"Hey, is this your dog?" came the question a few minutes later from yet another guy who was squatting in his own yard, playing with the same dog.

"No, but it seems to be following me."

"You want a Pepsi?" he asked.

"Sure!" I introduced myself to Steve and played with the friendly dog until Steve returned with two cold Pepsis.

"Well, she's got a collar, but no tag. You sure you don't want her? I already have eight dogs and I'm trying to get rid of some." This sounded ominous.

I thought about what it would be like to have a dog with me on my walk. I know absolutely *nothing* about dogs, and my apartment building doesn't even *allow* dogs this big. And what about our cat, Graciela?

But every time I looked at her I fell deeper into the dog-lover abyss.

"Maybe I should keep her," I heard myself saying.

Steve was sure she'd follow me, and he went off to fetch a leash and some dog food.

I kneeled down and asked her if she really wanted to walk across the

country with me. Looking closely at her collar I noticed that her name, Emmy, and a phone number were engraved on the buckle. I called the number and told the woman who answered that I was in Glazier and had her dog. Steve arranged to take Emmy to a neighbor who knew the owner.

I said goodbye to this beautiful little dog, Steve hugged me and gave me a blessing (in the name of Jesus), and I went on my way. Alone.

Objects Found Along the Road

Higgins, Texas   Day 80

"You're not planning to stay there, are you?"

I'd just set up my tent next to a barbed wire fence off the highway on a side road that seemed to lead to nowhere. But it must have led somewhere because here was this lady in her pickup who seemed to be upset I was planning to stay overnight.

"Well, it's a county road."

I could tell she wasn't happy. "Just make sure you don't go on the other side of that fence."

"Ma'am, I have no intention of climbing over that barbed wire fence." She drove off.

A while later her husband, pulled up in his pickup. "Where you headed?" He was friendly, and we chatted for a while. "My wife was ready to call the sheriff, but I told her to hold off till I talked to you."

Bill Hext is a local rancher whose home is just up the county road where I was camped. He returned a little later bearing grapes and carrot cake. I prefer chocolate cake to carrot cake, but I accepted his gifts graciously.

"How'd you like to go with me on my rounds in morning? I'll take you to breakfast."

No way I could refuse his offer. When would I ever have a chance to do something like this again?

"Sure! What time?"

He picked me up at 6 a.m. just as I'd finished packing up my gear in the dark. We drove to a rustic restaurant in Higgins where he treated me to French toast and eggs as Susie, Lennie, and other locals spoke about the weather and truck repairs. Then we were on our way.

Bill has several tracts of acreage in Texas and Oklahoma where he raises mostly cattle, but horses too. He's a few years younger than I and has been doing this his whole life. He'd also been a rodeo producer, and his granddaughter had been a prizewinning cowgirl when she was in middle school. The whole family is active in running the operation.

While we drove, Bill asked me three times what I thought about Donald Trump, and I refused to answer each time.

"I'll talk to you about God, money, the weather ... *anything* but politics." Finally, he gave up, and we talked about ranching, the ups and downs of the industry, and the role that oil has played in the lives of many landowners.

After entering each of his properties, he'd push a button on his dashboard activating a siren, and the animals would come out of nowhere to feed from the hay and feed he had in his truck. We fed and counted his several herds in both Texas and Oklahoma and even located a missing cow— turns out she'd just given birth to a calf and they were up on a near-by hill.

After feeding the cattle, we visited and fed his beautiful horses, who'd galloped up and surrounded the truck. I felt I was in the middle of a Western movie shoot.

Finally, we drove to a nearby feedlot, where many thousands of head of cattle are "finished and prepared" for market. It was quite a sight. And smell, too!

At 10 a.m. we were done. I grabbed my kart and thanked Bill for a once-in-a-lifetime experience. For him? He does this every day.

Arnett, Oklahoma   Day 81

March only has five more days to go out like a lamb, and it's not doing a very good job of it.

Last night I camped behind a collapsed wooden structure in a small field across from Perk's Convenience Store and the Church of the Nazarene.

Much of today was cold, overcast, wet, and windy. I wore four layers of clothing plus my rain jacket and pants, my merino wool cap,

and waterproof shoes. The problem is my gloves—they're too lightweight for the cold and not waterproof.

I entered Oklahoma this morning, and immediately the quality of the road deteriorated. There was only one motel in Arnett, and I'm in it. The room is warm and dry, and my gear is drying out.

Day 82   *Harmon, Oklahoma*

If I had any doubt that God is enjoying my journey, that was put to rest this morning.

Two days ago, a tackle box filled with lures showed up on the side of the road. This morning, 28 miles later, a fishing rod appeared.

As miserable as yesterday was, today was gorgeous and perfect for walking. Every field along the highway was filled with cattle and horses.

I was headed to Turkey Creek Lodge, which showed up on Google Maps. Its website featured a beautiful brick home and a glowing 5-star review. Sadly, it turned out to be bogus. The woman who answered the phone was surprised to get my call and warned me, "If you aren't legit, I'm armed!" She said she was in "the middle of renovating" and that the Web photo was just a "placeholder."

Finally, she asked, "Do you believe in God?" This was getting weirder.

"Yes, but I'm not a Christian," I replied.

"How can that be?" she asked.

"I'm Jewish," I answered.

"Well, Jesus was a Jew," she said.

"Yes. And Jesus worshipped the same God I do."

Apparently, she was satisfied with my explanation because she said I could stay.

But when I arrived later, no one was home except a horse and two dogs. The sorry-looking house sat in the middle of a yard filled with junk.

I may have fallen for her sham Bed and Breakfast, but it didn't cost me anything.

A mile up the road I found a great place to camp. Rain showers are predicted.

Vici, Oklahoma   **Day 83**

Last night, the sky delivered lightning, thunder, and plenty of rain, but I stayed dry atop my air mattress. (I was a 14-year-old Boy Scout the last time I was in a tent during a thunderstorm. That canvas tent had no floor and water came in from all sides in spite of the trenches we'd dug around the perimeter. Everything was soaked, including us.)

The Morford House Bed & Breakfast in Vici (locally pronounced "Vigh-sigh") does not provide breakfast, "but you'll have kitchen privileges. And we only accept cash." It's a lovely old home, with polished wood floors and a remodeled kitchen and bathrooms. I'm up a flight of narrow stairs in a tiny bedroom with one twin bed.

Just what I needed.

Day 84   *Seiling, Oklahoma*

Vici was enveloped in a dense fog as I departed early in the morning. I proceeded with extreme caution.

Traffic crept along, and the first hour was tedious as I moved on and off the narrow shoulder. ("Be safe!")

As the sun broke through and burned off the haze, I remained on alert during the 21-mile, nine-hour walk to Seiling.

"My daughter uses Facebook and all that stuff," said Geneva, who'd gotten out of her car to chat and then handed me some cash.

Later at the Seiling Motel, Sheryl and Vance comped my room for the night. It's a clean, efficient, well-run motel. I recommend that you stop by when you're in Seiling.

Tonight is the first night of Passover. There is no Seder to attend, but in honor of the holiday I ate my tuna sub before sundown. Sharon's care package containing matzoh will arrive in a day or two.

Artist of the Day: Dave McKenna, well-known for his "three-handed" swing style: a walking bassline, mid-range chords, and an improvised melody. Simply incredible!

Highway 60, Oklahoma **Day 85**

When I see road construction, I try to "walk where they ain't"—often down the center of the median. Today no one was working, so I walked on the dirt road used for construction vehicles.

Along the way I encountered a community Easter egg hunt and heard a snatch of "Beer Barrel Polka." Inspired by the polka music, I listened to Big Lou, the Accordion Princess's *Polka Casserole*. We've had the pleasure of meeting and hearing Big Lou in San Francisco.

Other than cans, bottles, miscellaneous trash, and plastic bags filled with cans, bottles, and miscellaneous trash, the items I see most often on the side of the road are work gloves. I see gloves all day long.

Later the sheriff pulled over and asked where I was headed. He offered me a ride, which I declined. He said, "If you need help just call the sheriff's office."

I'm camped on a county road. I hear cows, but no freight trains.

Day 86   *Fairview, Oklahoma*

It was *cold* today! I put my rain gear on just to cut the frigid wind.

Once again, my gloves didn't do the job; every time I took them off to take a photo or check my phone, my fingers just "turned to ice."

I listened to an interesting interview of Ira Glass, 59, the host of *This American Life.* He referred to himself as "old" several times, which is laughable.

One thing Glass said that I could relate to was not wanting to be bored in his job. Another was his willingness to seek out and try to understand people with different backgrounds, religious beliefs, and political views, things I'm challenged to do each day of my journey.

Today a nice woman stopped her pickup truck and asked, "Do you need a ride?" I took off my glove to shake her hand and she remarked at how cold my hand was. Then she gave me some cash. "Here, let me buy you lunch!"

At the Best Western, Daisy greeted me and handed me the packages Sharon had mailed. They contained shoes, a shirt, my Gordini ski gloves, and matzoh.

Observing Passover on the road is a challenge, but I'm trying. (Did you know that Triscuits do not contain leaven? Just whole grain wheat, canola oil, and sea salt.)

I spent the afternoon sitting in the Jacuzzi, eating Triscuits and thawing out.

Ringwood, Oklahoma   Day 87

Finally my hands were warm. The Gordini gloves made all the difference.

Around lunchtime, I saw a lawn sign that said, "Martha Brown, Tax Services," and I pushed my kart onto the edge of a driveway. As I ate, a woman drove down the driveway, stopped, and rolled down her window.

"Why don't you go sit in my husband's truck over there and get out of the wind."

I asked if she was Martha, which she indeed was. "I think I'll take you up on that!" As she drove off, I got into the old Chevy truck and ate in comfort.

Twenty minutes later, Martha invited me into her home office where I met her husband, Percy, and their Schnauzer, Sassy.

Martha does tax returns during the tax season. Percy is a tractor mechanic and a professional restorer of classic tractors. I admired their extensive collection of model cars displayed in the office.

It turns out that Martha knows many people and everyone respects her. After we became Facebook friends, a number of her family members, friends, and friends-of-friends began following my journey. And I was happy to welcome them all!

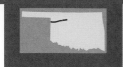

Day 88

Enid, Oklahoma

Blowing at 30 to 40 mph, the wind was pushing me forward and to the right. Was it trying to drive me off the road or just blow me down?

Today I was walking *with* traffic (not usually advisable), because that's where the shoulder was much wider. Twice the kart almost blew over.

A woman honked her horn and waved as she pulled up in front of me. It was Jana Brown, the daughter of Martha and Percy whom I'd met the day before. I climbed into her warm car and she told me about her job teaching history at Northwestern Oklahoma State University while working on her doctorate at OSU. Jana is quite knowledgeable about local and state history.

After struggling against the wind for another 10 miles, I was offered a ride and I took it! Robert (in his mid-80s) and I lifted my kart into his truck and he drove me 7 miles to my motel, where I noticed that the flagpole had blown over.

Starting at midnight there is a Wind Advisory in effect, with gusts of 40 to 57 mph, as well as a Freeze Warning, with temperatures dropping into the 20's.

Pond Creek, Oklahoma   Day 89

As rough as it was yesterday, today was a beautiful day to walk!

The sun was shining all day, the wind remained under 10 mph, and I walked 25 miles.

My room features the wood paneling one only sees in such vintage, small-town motels. But it's clean, the fixtures and appliances are up-to-date, and the Wi-Fi seems better than in many chain motels.

The *Radio Lab* Podcast of the Day was the story of the first female gondolier in Venice, and featured a surprise ending to this fascinating story.

At McDonalds I had a second breakfast and chatted with a bunch of "seniors" (just like me). They asked about my journey, and one guy, wearing a Korean War Veteran cap, asked how old I was. When I told him, he laughed, "Only 71? *Ha!*"

Objects Found Along the Road

Ponca City, Oklahoma

Days 90–91

I walked hard today knowing that tomorrow would bring an extreme temperature drop into the low 20's, with rain, thunderstorms, and sleet expected.

I'd already walked 23 miles when Eric pulled up, asked if I was okay, and offered me a lift.

I told him I'd love to take him up on the offer, but I was headed toward Ponca City. He replied that he'd be going there after he picked up his kids.

When he came back, we lifted my kart into the bed of his truck and bonded on the fact that we both do pull-ups. He's a firefighter and ambulance tech.

I met three of his four children, Thaddeus, Declan, and Bella (playing second base tonight for the Firecrackers).

Arriving at the YMCA ball field, Eric handed me a jar of homemade peach jam, a gift from his wife, Angela. As I walked toward town, Angela drove by and she and daughter Abigail came over to chat. What a sweet family!

The Inn where I'd made a reservation for two nights turned out to be a dump! The whole place looked and smelled worse than I could have imagined. I left and walked another mile to America's Best Value Inn where, for the same price, I now have a decent room in which to spend the next two nights as I wait out the storm.

I was assured by several Oklahomans that the weather will improve soon.

At noon the following day I was still waiting for the precipitation, but it hadn't come. My body and brain both needed and deserved a rest, but staying in a motel is a mixed blessing. My neighbors were partying, and I had to call the front desk twice. By 10 a.m. they were gone. Being in my tent is often a welcome relief from real life.

By evening, there was light rain, a drop in temperature, gustier wind, and another prediction of sleet and snow by morning.

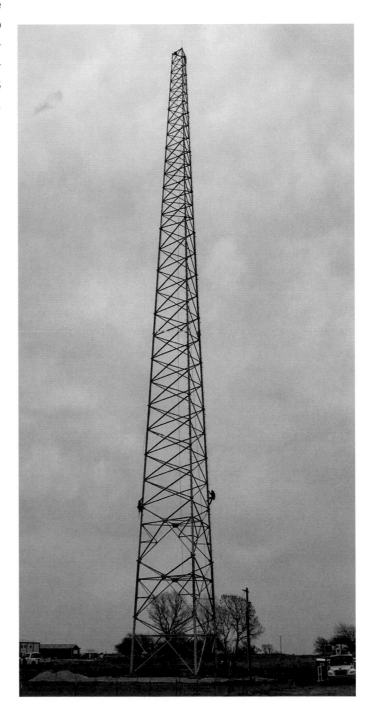

Shidler, Oklahoma   Day 92

Tonight I was in a race with the setting sun. The sun won.

The promise of snow finally arrived early this morning, leaving its evidence on the windows of vehicles parked in the motel lot.

It wasn't a difficult walk today; it was just a *long* walk, 27 miles and 11 hours on the road. With no appropriate place to set up my tent, I just kept walking until it was dark and finally set up on a county road off Hwy 60 close to wind turbines and oil rigs. Trucks passed by all night, but no one paid any attention to me.

Day 93   *Pawhuska, Oklahoma*

This morning I encountered hail the size of baseballs! Well, more the size of couscous. But with a cold headwind, it wasn't fun.

As I've said many times, this country is built for driving, not walking.

Pawhuska is typical of many Southwest towns—ranching, farming, railroad. The Osage tribal government has been based here since 1872.

Artist of the Day: Barney Kessel was an early jazz hero of mine—I nearly wore out the grooves on his LPs when I was a young, aspiring jazz guitarist.

In 1944, Kessel was the only white musician featured in the acclaimed short jazz film *Jammin' the Blues*. All that was clearly visible of him were his hands, which had been dyed black.

He had a long career as a touring artist and studio musician and was an early member of the famed "Wrecking Crew."

I finally got to meet Barney in person in 1981 at the King of France Tavern, an Annapolis jazz club. He invited me to sit with him at the bar while he ate steak and drank white wine. For 5 minutes we talked about music. Then, for another 15 minutes, we talked about our recent divorces.

Highway 60, Oklahoma **Day 94**

At 2 p.m. I was taking a break and saw a few small drops of water on my phone. And then my jacket sleeve. And my pants. I looked up and the sun was shining. I checked the weather app: 0% chance of precipitation all day. I thought, okay, a few drops, an anomaly. It'll pass.

As I resumed walking, I put on my rain jacket as the anomalous drops increased and the sun disappeared behind clouds.

As the downpour began, I ran while pushing my kart across a grass field toward a mound of broken concrete and rebar off to the side of the highway. Once there I set up my tent and rain fly as fast as I could!

I then spent a restful afternoon alone in my tent in the Oklahoma rain.

Since I'm in Osage country, I listened to Terry Gross's interview with David Grann, author of *Killers of the Flower Moon: The Osage Murders and the Birth of the FBI*. It's a fascinating story about conspiracy and murder.

Day 95   *Bartlesville, Oklahoma*

After a cold but restful night camped behind broken concrete and re-bar, I dodged traffic all morning while wondering if I could sue the idiots who designed a highway with a 1-inch shoulder.

Bartlesville (pop. 36,595) is the longtime home of Phillips Petroleum Company. In 1905 Frank Phillips founded the company here that would later become Phillips 66 and ConocoPhillips. The downtown is a vibrant little city, with nice sidewalks. But then the sidewalks disappeared. Same old problem.

Fresh Air Podcast of the Day: "How Rodgers & Hammerstein Revolutionized Broadway." Terry Gross interviewed Todd Purdum, author of *Something Wonderful: Rodgers and Hammerstein's Broadway Revolution.*

The background music at IHOP was so obnoxious and irritating that I told the hostess I wanted my lunch to go. I brought it back to my motel room and ate in peace.

Nowata, Oklahoma   Day 96

Today's walk was nerve-wracking and generally unsafe.

I wandered between store and church parking lots, between the road and the grass, and on occasional sidewalks for miles.

Crossing into Nowata County the road improved and lasted for seven miles before it was back to a 1-inch shoulder and even heavier truck traffic.

Then there were flashing lights ahead.

The Oklahoma Highway Patrol officer was polite, friendly, and concerned. He even expressed regret that the shoulder was inadequate, blah, blah. In the end, he ordered me to only walk on the grass, *not* the road.

"Yes, officer, absolutely!" *In your dreams!* There was no way I could manage to push my kart for miles through the grass and weeds and up and down embankments while avoiding drainage ditches, trash, and other obstacles. When he was out of sight I got back on the highway. But I really needed to escape this miserable, dangerous highway.

In Nowata, Daniel, manager of the Rudd Motel (and also a musician—thank you, God), agreed to give me a lift the next day.

Just what the Oklahoma Highway Patrol ordered.

Days 97–98

Big Cabin, Oklahoma

At 5 a.m. Jana Brown sent me a text warning of scary weather and possible tornadoes. I began to entertain the possibility of my demise in a tornado.

Daniel and I loaded the kart into his SUV and we drove to Big Cabin. Along the way he talked about growing up in Nowata and his years touring and gigging on guitar and bass and performing rock, country, and the Red Dirt music popular in Oklahoma.

As we drove I observed the highway shoulder, which at times was 8-centimeters wide.

The motel manager checked me in early, and fighting a really strong wind, I crossed the highway to the truck stop where I ordered a tuna wrap instead of the usual sub. A nice change.

In response to the weather prediction of rain, hail, tornadoes, locusts, and frogs, I decided to hole up for two nights.

After breakfast the following morning, I emptied my kart, refolded my clothes, rearranged everything, and took it easy. I walked across the highway again for lunch and then spent a few hours on Google Maps deciding where to head next. Based on the estimated size of road shoulders, I decided to go *north*.

A Tornado Watch remains in effect, but the local weather has been decent. I soaked in the Jacuzzi for a while and rested some more.

Tonight the evening sky was a particular shade of yellow that I cannot recall ever having seen before.

Afton, Oklahoma   Day 99

I wore five layers of clothing as I walked on this cold, windy, overcast, gray day. A strong tailwind pushed me along. I barely took a break—it was just too cold to sit down.

Afton, a town of just over 1,000 people, is tucked into the extreme upper right corner of Oklahoma. While walking across the Horse Creek bridge, I felt for a moment like I was in Mayberry.

During its Route 66 heyday, the downtown was probably humming with hotels, businesses, cars, and people. But today it's mostly empty shells and boarded-up buildings.

The only motel in town still open is the one I'm in, the Route 66 Motel. When I checked in, I got the impression I was the only guest.

The room is tired, but it's clean, the water is hot and plentiful, and there's a microwave and fridge. For some reason there are illustrations of zebras and leopards on the walls.

Just right for someone who's walked 27 miles.

Day 100   *Miami, Oklahoma*

The Miami Days Inn has a Jacuzzi, and I was sitting in it five minutes after checking in. The wind and cold were *wicked* and never let up all day.

Freeze warnings are in effect for tonight through tomorrow, with temperatures in the 20's predicted. (I plan to not leave my room until the temp gets up at least into the 30's.)

On my way to the city of Miami (pop. 13,570), there was no law enforcement visible; but I did come across a beautiful snake. Soon I'll be heading north into Kansas and then heading east to Missouri, Highway 50, and hopefully a better walking route.

Baxter Springs, Kansas **Day 101**

I'm in Mickey Mantle country.

Mickey grew up in nearby Commerce and began his pro baseball career playing for the Baxter Springs Whiz Kids. Sadly, I no longer own his baseball card, and this is as close to the great Mantle as I'll ever be. (Disclosure: We were *not* Yankees fans in my house.)

The Rose Cottage in Baxter Springs (pop. 4,238) is a lovely B&B guest house filled with antiques, period items, and Route 66 memorabilia. The owner, Jane, is friendly and hospitable, and I enjoyed talking to her. She has a married daughter who lives in my birthplace, Brooklyn, NY (the reason why we weren't Yankees fans).

On the map, it appears I'm almost at the very center of the US. But the true geographical center belongs to Lebanon, KS, about 370 miles to the northwest.

Day 102   *Pittsburg, Kansas*

"My grandson lost his cell phone along here last night. Have you seen it?"

I told the man in the pickup truck that I hadn't, but I'd take his cell number and keep an eye out for it. Ten minutes later I called him.

"Tom, I've got good news and bad news." I'd found the phone, but it was smushed. When he came back, he thanked me and said, "I suppose this is better than having all the data stolen." I guess.

Later while walking and talking to Sharon on the phone, Officer Reddy of the Kansas Highway Patrol pulled up. We talked about my walk and our exercise workouts, and he put me into the KHP computer system. Not for the first time, I have law enforcement looking out for me.

While looking for a place to camp overnight, I saw a perfectly good cemetery, but passed it by.

A couple of miles later, just past the Kansas Crossing Casino & Hotel, I spied a lot dominated by a tall mound of asphalt. Camped behind the 20-foot mound I was totally invisible from the highway. And in spite of the background din of traffic, I heard some beautiful birdsongs to listen to as I watched a lovely sunset.

Pittsburg, Kansas   # Day 103

I woke up to the sound of a bulldozer.

The driver was loading asphalt from the nearby pile into a truck. He paid no attention to me as I packed up my gear. I made a wide arc around the dozer and headed onto the highway.

I'd *happily* camp behind a mound of rocks or asphalt *every* night if I could. Trees and vegetation may be prettier, but when you're sleeping along the highway, nothing beats a mound of asphalt.

I estimate that I've now walked over 1,500 miles, more than halfway to the Atlantic.

Arriving at the Pittsburg Super 8 before noon, I ate lunch, gave myself a haircut and beard trim, took a shower, and then took a nap.

Later, after replenishing supplies (fruit, protein bars, water, yogurt), I picked up a fish dinner at Long John Silver's. The fish was pretty good and came with two tasty hush puppies, which I always thought were shoes.

My body turns everything I eat directly into energy, and I'm probably in as ideal physical shape as I've ever been. This window of self-indulgence, however, will be brief.

Day 104   *Fort Scott, Kansas*

Fort Scott seems like a nice town, but I'll always remember it as the place where my tooth broke.

I walked past major road construction all day long. One of the construction supervisors, Ben, drove by to check out my kart and offered me a bottle of cold chocolate milk. Each little bottle contains *two* servings. Ha! As if some construction worker—or *anyone*—would drink half a bottle of chocolate milk today and save the other half for tomorrow.

On the road I found a wallet containing $5 and a young man's ID; later I picked up a small pouch containing insulin syringes.

After hearing about my walk, the front desk clerk upgraded me to a top floor mini-suite at no extra charge. I gave her the wallet, including the $5, and she said she'd take care of it.

While eating an apple after supper, I cracked a tooth. My dentist warned me this would happen, and she was right. I'll need yet another crown, but can't really have this done while I'm on the road. So an emergency visit to a local dentist was called for.

Prescott, Kansas   Day 105

I called Fort Scott Family Dental at 7:30 a.m. After explaining my unusual situation to Carina, she put me on hold while she called the dentist at his home. After coming back on the line she said, "Dr. Crawford is picking you up at the motel. He'll be there in five minutes." (Frankly, I *still* can't believe this.)

Dr. Tim Crawford is pleasant, young, and affable. Driving to his office, we talked the whole way. I learned that he and his wife have five kids, he's Canadian, and she is from the Midwest.

Carina gave me forms to fill out, contacted my insurance company, and assured me they'd work it all out.

As Karis, the dental assistant, prepped me, I asked if the office had a way to dispose of used syringes. She took the batch of needles I'd found on the road the day before, and Ashley, another assistant, assured me she'd properly dispose of them.

Dr. Crawford was soon working on my tooth, and in short order I had my temporary filling. (My own dentist later admired his work.)

Then Carina drove me back to my motel! *Can you believe this?*

I am truly blessed. The weather today was beautiful, the road perfect, and I walked 17 miles today—*after* the trip to the dentist.

Days 106–107

La Cygne, Kansas

I awoke to traffic sounds, songbirds, and a nearby train whistle. Wait! Wasn't it supposed to be raining? Ten seconds later the sound of raindrops joined the soundtrack.

The rain soon ended and I was back on the road heading north. Because there's no place to stealth camp along Highway 69, I walked an extra three miles to Linn County Park and Marina. Entering the park, raindrops again began to fall. I asked a couple in a red pickup for directions to the campsites.

"Just keep walking on this road." They drove off, but two minutes later they were back, offering me a ride. And more. Not only did Rick and Tina lend a hand pitching my tent, but Rick insisted on paying the campsite fee! They and their dog, Wally, are my latest angels. That night, I fell asleep to the sounds of ducks, geese, songbirds, and the calming rain.

The following morning it was rain and more rain. I stayed in my tent, which did a pretty good job keeping things dry; but over two days the rain somehow finds its way in.

At 6 p.m. the second night the sun finally came out.

Louisburg, Kansas   **Day 108**

After a hot shower in the well-heated bathhouse, I was ready to resume my journey, walking in the bright sun that had finally come out.

Todd Peach has been a friend for over 20 years, although we'd never met. We became acquainted through his website, which features the lyrics of Frank Sinatra and Ella Fitzgerald recordings.

Todd and his wife Sharon live in Seattle, and our travels happened to intersect right here at a Highway 69 exit ramp. He arrived with Subway sandwiches, chips, and a Dr Pepper, and we talked of many things.

Through the Couchsurfing app, I connected with Kaleb Kasitz. Although Kaleb no longer lives in Louisburg, his family does, and they

welcomed me into their home for the night. Parents Rodney, a retired teacher, and Leanne, a veterinarian, cooked up a delicious dinner of fish, rice, corn, fresh broccoli, and pickled beets. Their son Marcus, a network engineer, joined us.

The generosity of strangers is not lost on me.

Day 109   *Stillwell, Kansas*

On my way to Stilwell, two Miami County deputy sheriffs, Colin and Andrew, stopped and asked if I was okay. Later I met Sue Goodman, who knows the Kasitz family (and just about everyone!) who also stopped to see if I was okay.

After six hours of walking, I made a stop at the Stilwell Animal Hospital & Equine Center, the clinic of Leanne Landau Kasitz, DVM. It's an impressive brick building inside and out and where I'd take our cat, Graciela, if we lived here. Leanne was out, but Marcus was holding down the fort.

A few miles later I arrived at the home of Deb Mitchell, whom I met through the WarmShowers cycling app. She's a project manager and her husband John is a product engineer.

They prepared an excellent dinner of salmon, a lentil and rice dish, corn, avocado, and salad. (Fish two nights in a row!) We talked for hours.

Lee's Summit, Missouri　Day 110

This morning, after John dropped me off at a spot he said would be safer to push my kart, I walked through a rain that had been falling steadily for hours.

It wasn't a debilitating rain, but I was glad to be dressed in rain jacket, rain pants, and waterproof shoes. At Highway 291, I turned north.

When I arrived at the Lee's Summit Super 8, my room was not ready, so I hung out in the lobby and caught up on social media. As soon as I could, I stashed my gear and walked to a nearby grocery store and stocked up on soup, tuna, bananas, cheese, bread, protein bars, and snacks.

In 2010, CNN/Money and Money magazine ranked Lee's Summit 27th on its list of the "100 Best Cities to Live in the United States." The city is *not* named for Robert E. Lee. Rather, it's named after a man named Lea. They misspelled it a few times and it finally stuck. Guitarist Pat Metheny is from here.

After heading north for days, I'll finally be moving east again tomorrow on Hwy 50, sometimes referred to as "The Loneliest Road."

Day 111   *Pittsville, Missouri*

The Loneliest Highway is not lonely at all. In fact, it could be called "The Noisiest Highway," and for an hour or so I walked on a parallel road, The Blue Parkway, to avoid the noise and congestion.

In keeping with the cinematic drama of my journey, a dozen sheriff's cars, sirens flashing and blaring, sped by heading east. One of those cars returned and an armed deputy jumped out and yelled, "Have you seen anyone walking along the highway?"

"No, but if I do, who should I call?"

"911!" he shouted.

"Okay! Male? Female?"

"Male—with tattoos!"

"Got it!" I replied, as he and his partner sped away.

In the movie version of my journey, I spy the tattooed guy hiding along the road and I'm instrumental in his capture. But in real life I didn't see anyone walking, besides myself.

Later I met James (male, with tattoos) who drives a Google Maps camera vehicle. I asked him about my route, but he didn't have any great suggestions. He just said I should walk facing traffic and added, "Be safe!"

After 18 miles I began looking for a suitable camping site, but saw nothing. Finally, I found a field that looked promising. The gate was open. I removed my reflective vest and made my move.

Although I'm somewhat exposed, this was the best I could do. In its defense, I'm under a clear blue sky and the birds are singing.

I must be getting close to St. Louis—I just heard and saw the most beautiful red cardinal sitting in a nearby tree!

Warrensburg, Missouri **Day 112**

I love Mel Brooks.

Today I listened to Mel tell interviewer Marc Maron that when he was a teenager he worked as a waiter and entertainer at Butler Lodge in the Catskills. I perked up! My maternal grandfather, Samuel Adler, used to go to Butler Lodge all the time, and I have no doubt he saw the young Mel Brooks there.

My Grandpa was a widower. He never remarried, but my cousins and I always wondered if he had any girlfriends. He was a very cool guy, with a cigarette holder, a classic comb over, and a little lapel pin from the Ishbitzer Benevolent Society. Grandpa would play the card game Casino with me for hours.

At a convenience store along Hwy 50 I chatted with Carie, a young woman who was working the counter. She showed me a photo of her little pig who is now the mascot of the local sheriff's department. She then gave me a can of sliced pineapple from her own private stash.

A little while later I chatted with Joe, who was watering a flower bed at the Hunter Heirloom Quilting store. Before I left he asked if he could pray for me. I always welcome prayers, but warned him that I'm Jewish. Joe paused for just a second, put his arms around me, and closed his eyes as he began his blessing, invoking "The Lord" instead of Jesus. I still marvel how thoughtful, sensitive, and considerate this was.

Day 113   *Sedalia, Missouri*

The woman making my tuna sub was taking a painfully long time, and I was hungry! I was at a Casey's General Store (they're located adjacent to gas stations).

She finally began wrapping it up, but changed her mind. I watched in slow-motion as she tossed a perfectly good tuna sub, with lettuce, tomato, Swiss cheese, and cucumber into the trash. As it was in the air I yelled, *No!* But it was too late. She told me it was "too sloppy," and proceeded to make an entirely new sub from scratch.

I sighed and waited *another* 10 minutes as she displayed her sandwich artistry. It was all I could do to not grab the old sub out of the trash.

Later I listened to a podcast about California's efforts to ban plastic drinking straws. People should only see what I see as I walk along our nation's littered highways.

After almost 11 hours and 26 miles on the road, I arrived at Sedalia. It was a long day, but the shoulder was fine, as was the weather.

Tipton, Missouri   Day 114

The Scott Joplin Memorial Highway is a lovely section of Hwy 50 that features tree-lined streets with grand homes and sidewalks. Joplin moved to Sedalia in 1894, played at local social clubs, and began composing music. Although he only lived here for seven years, it was long enough to get a mile-long section of highway named after him in 2016.

As I walked under a cloudless blue sky, I listened to Marc Maron's entertaining interviews of actor Eugene Levy *(Waiting for Guffman, A Mighty Wind)* and actor/director Ron Howard.

The claim to fame of Tipton (pop. 3,378) is a water tower painted to look like an eight ball. The tower originated in 1968 when native son Ewald Fischer established what became the largest builder of pool tables in the US. The company was bought and sold a few times, and the water tower was painted over. But Tipton eventually got its tower restored. It's generally regarded as the world's largest eight ball.

Day 115 *Jefferson City, Missouri*

The stretch of Hwy 50 before and after Tipton is, frankly, treacherous and scary, with a broken, narrow pavement and heavy traffic. So when I checked into the Twin Pine Motel I asked Rocky (whose family owns it) if he'd give me a lift out of town in the morning.

So, after a 15 minute drive, I exited his car, reassembled my kart, and headed east. The weather has turned warmer. April, rather than March, is going out like a lamb.

Bruce, a Missouri highway patrol officer, stopped, chatted, and wished me luck, thanking me for my father's service during WWII.

At Jefferson City, the capital of Missouri, I walked along Missouri St. to the Baymont Inn & Suites, where my room had a view of the capitol building.

I spent the afternoon looking at a map of the Katy Trail. I plan to walk a 100-mile section from Jefferson City to St. Charles.

Tebbetts, Missouri   **Day 116**

The first time I stayed at a hostel was the summer of 1974 in Vancouver after I'd taken the Canadian National Railroad from Montreal. Today was the second time.

The Katy Trail Turner Shelter is a similar hostel and costs *(drum roll ...)* $6 a night.

After a memorable walk over the Missouri River, I reached the Katy trailhead. The trail is made of hard-packed limestone pug (crushed limestone) and is suitable for bikes and my kart.

The first cyclist I met on the Trail was Ron Gossen, a retired business professor, who's cycling across the state. (He was the first person who advised me *not* to walk across St. Louis.) We exchanged contact information and later became friends.

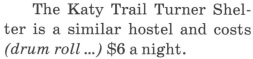

I walked all day to the Turner Shelter where I was later joined by four cyclists traveling together.

Kim and Kevin, Eva, and Maureen are fun and interesting. As we ate dinner we shared stories about being on the road.

When everyone was in his or her bunk and the lights were turned out, there was a small crash on the far side of the room. Somebody asked, "What was that?" Somebody else answered, "Nothing. I just dropped my Glock."

Good to know someone's carrying.

Day 117

Bluffton, Missouri

On the Katy Trail today, I had the odd experience of being recognized by several strangers greeting me by name. Word about a guy named Robert pushing a kart across America had somehow spread.

A Chicago couple, Jim and Mary, had eaten breakfast that morning with Ron, the retired professor. And Kevin, a young man hiking the Katy Trail carrying a backpack, was at The Barn B&B when I'd called this morning to make a reservation.

I'd recently read Stephen Ambrose's book about the Lewis and Clark expedition, and today I walked along the Missouri River (it really *is* wide!).

The owner of a small grocery store along the trail has garnered some poor online reviews for being inhospitable to cyclists, as well as for being a grump.

Personally, I did not find him grumpy. Rather, he was an easy racist, injecting into our short conversation facts about which black men in town were living with white women; a short history of slavery in the region; and that many people in the next county had long, unpronounceable German names. "They are not regular white people like you and me."

Needless to say, I did not reveal my secret identity. I just paid for my Moon Pie, Snickers, and Dr Pepper and got the hell out of there.

Later, after eating dinner with Doug, the amiable host of The Barn B&B, I settled into bed.

INSTRUCTIONS IN CASE OF AN EMERGENCY

WE CARE ABOUT YOUR SAFETY

ENTERING A NUCLEAR POWER PLANT EMERGENCY PLANNING ZONE

The health and safety of the public is our top priority. Warning sirens are installed in the area in case of threatening weather conditions, an emergency at Ameren Missouri's Callaway Energy Center, or any other public safety condition.

If the sirens sound, you may find additional emergency information at the following locations:
- Tune your radio to KTXY 106.9 FM or other local stations
- Visit http://Ameren.com on the web
- Follow @Ameren Missouri on Twitter or Ameren Missouri's Facebook page

If you do not hear or find any messages at the above locations, you should leave the area immediately while observing all traffic laws for your safety. Call 911 if you need assistance.

SIRENS ARE TESTED ON THE FIRST TUESDAY OF EACH MONTH AT APPROXIMATELY 12:00 NOON.

Posted by the Missouri State Emergency Management Agency

Hermann, Missouri   **Day 118**

There was quite a thunderstorm in the early morning hours, and as I walked, the sky remained cloudy and gray.

I decided to stay overnight in Hermann (pop. 2,431), which was founded in 1837 by the Deutsche Ansiedlungs-Gesellschaft zu Philadelphia. Before Prohibition, it was a major wine producing area and currently calls itself the sausage-making capital of Missouri.

Although the main road into town is lined with charming guest houses and B&Bs, I walked to the city park and for $15 set up my tent on a grassy spot near a creek.

When I walked to Hardee's across the highway and ordered a fish sandwich, the kid said, "We're out of fish until next year." To add insult to injury, they were also out of Dr Pepper "until tomorrow." I settled for a Cherry Coke, which may be Warren Buffett's favorite drink, but what does he know?

Day 119   *Marthasville, Missouri*

After exiting the park I somehow got turned around. Because it was cloudy, I couldn't see the sun and headed in the wrong direction. Worse still, I was pushing the kart up a steep hill. Finally checking my compass app, I realized my mistake and wasted a lot of time and energy returning to my starting point. (The same thing happened to Lewis and Clark more than once.)

I was exhausted by the time I walked from Hermann to Treloar. Once again there was no place to stay or camp.

At the visitor information display I saw a couple looking at the exhibit describing Daniel Boone's presence and influence in the region. I introduced myself to Bruce and Susie and then brazenly asked if they'd be willing to give me a five-minute ride to Marthasville, where the Katy Trail guidebook indicated it was okay to camp for free.

"Sure," Bruce said.

"Why not?" said Susie.

And a few minutes later we were there. I set up the tent in a secluded spot under a tree.

Bruce and Susie Tippit are from Miami, Oklahoma. He's a retired firefighter, and she is a retired RN who shares a bloodline with Daniel Boone. Add two more angels to my growing list.

Defiance, Missouri

Day 120

I'd planned to spend tonight in a "primitive" campsite in Klondike Park. But after climbing a steep hill I was dismayed to find that every tent site was reserved. Frustrated, I climbed back down the slope and continued walking.

I called the Katy Trail information number for the next town, Defiance, and spoke to Robin, the owner of the Katy Bike Rental shop. She invited me to pitch my tent on the lawn behind her shop. Now *that's* hospitality!

On my way, Rebecca at the Pop-A-Wheelie Café made me a two-egg sandwich with Mexican cheese and spinach on an everything bagel, plus a *delicious* fruit and yogurt smoothie.

Teri and Hunter welcomed me to the bike shop, where I pitched my tent and listened to the live music coming from a nearby bar/restaurant. The songs all featured three chords, unintelligible lyrics, a heavy backbeat, and an abundance of cymbal crashes. These guys may have more powerful amps than I did when I was 16, but I knew more chords.

Today I listened to *Peter and the Wolf* by Prokofiev, who also knew more than three chords.

Day 121   *St. Charles, Missouri*

I only had to walk 8.4 miles today to reach my motel in St. Charles (what a slacker). But it rained this morning, so my tent and some other stuff were wet.

The sun was shining when I arrived at the Wingate, and I immediately started doing laundry after hanging my wet gear on the shower rod and closet doors.

My friend Gerry Mandel, who lives in St. Louis, came by at 3:30 p.m. with a package Sharon had sent for me. Sharon and I met Gerry and his wife MaryLee during a trip to China years ago, and it was good to see him again. When Gerry asked what else he could bring, I told him "oranges and bananas," which he brought.

I loved walking on the Katy Trail, especially where it followed the course of the Missouri River.

Aviston, Illinois   # Day 122

The Schoen Theory of Decision Making says:

The more difficult a decision is to make, the less important it is which alternative you take.

During the last few days I've been driving myself nuts trying to decide whether I should continue east on Highway 50 or Highway 40. I've spent hours on Google Maps, looking at the width of each road's shoulder as it meanders across the map. Both highways merge on

and off with Interstates, which I avoid. The shoulders are intermittently wide or nonexistent for miles at a time.

Jeff Rudisill summed it up, saying, "Well, Bob, it looks to me like either road will work for you, and each has its advantages and disadvantages." In the end, I could have just flipped a coin.

Now it was time to have breakfast with Ron Gossen, who would be driving me across St. Louis. After eating, we drove past Busch Stadium, the zoo, and the Arch and then drove through East St. Louis and the shells of some formerly glorious buildings.

Ron dropped me off on Highway 50 in Illinois, and I walked 13 miles under a cloudless sky to the Eagle Inn, where I soaked in the Jacuzzi and then went to sleep.

Day 123   *Carlyle, Illinois*

I finally had an encounter with a tick. But as I would find out later, that was the least of my problems.

After walking to Carlyle, I was eating lunch at the desk in my motel room and noticed the tick on my outer thigh. While it wasn't embedded in my skin, it was close to the site of a number of bites I hadn't noticed before. I grabbed it, put it in a cup of water, and took a shower. By the time I'd finished my shower the tick had climbed out of the water and was on the rim of the cup. I stuck it back in the water and examined my legs more closely. I saw no ticks, but there were many more bites present on the backs of my thighs. And they were itching.

By now, the tick was out of the water again, and I just flushed the sucker.

Now I was paranoid, wondering whether I would succumb to Lyme disease, or worse.

The truth was simpler: I was a victim of bedbugs that had been hiding in the upholstered desk chair. The tick was, simply, a red herring.

Salem, Illinois　　Day 124

Today was a double challenge. Rain and itching. I can't do much about the rain, but Benadryl cream is on its way.

It rained incessantly, and the gravel shoulder was frustrating. I was on and off US 50 for hours. Eventually the sun came out and the shoulder got wider, and when I reached the town of Sandoval there was finally a sidewalk.

In total I walked 23 miles to the Salem Days Inn, where I was well taken care of by the friendly owners, Sam and his wife Trupti. She did my laundry as a special favor since there's no guest laundry.

Salem (pop. 7,485) was the birthplace of William Jennings Bryan.

Objects Found Along the Road

Flora, Illinois   Days 125–126

The distance from Salem to Flora was 28 miles, and it took 13 hours of walking. Had I seen an appropriate spot to camp at a halfway point, I'd have stopped. But I didn't, so I just kept walking.

I've now walked over 1,900 miles and am closer to my destination than I'd realized.

John Bayler, who manages the US Route 50 Walkers, Bikers and Travelers Facebook page, was sitting in his white pickup waiting for me. As I approached he came out to greet me, carrying an SLR camera.

John had noticed me walking and wanted to get my story and a photo, which he later posted on Facebook.

My back, hips, and legs took a beating today, so I decided to stay two nights at the Best Western.

Early to bed and early to rise means an early breakfast, like 6 a.m.

I ate Raisin Bran with milk, a banana, blueberries, and chocolate chips; an English Muffin with cream cheese and strawberry jam; a tangerine; orange juice and my vitamins. I grabbed a yogurt for later.

Plumbing noises from the bathroom prompted a move to a quieter (and bigger) room down the hall. (Sharon *hates* to change motel rooms, but not me! She says that's because I never take anything out of my suitcase.)

As I was obsessing on Google Maps, I got a text from John Bayler inviting me to lunch at the NMN Club (the letters mean *No More Nicotine*). John's friend Debbie joined us, and she told the incredible story of finding her birth family. After lunch, John drove me around town, showing me local industries and parks.

I've decided to make Rehoboth Beach, Delaware, my final destination.

Olney, Illinois   Day 127

I've learned that my day goes best when I get a really early start. So that's what I did today.

I was on the road by 5:40 a.m. and walked 22.7 miles to the Super 8 in Olney. There's a Burger King next door where I just had a fish sandwich, fries, a non-caffeinated root beer, and some kind of Hershey's dessert pie. Keep those calories, protein, and fat coming my way!

Unfortunately, the flies were out in force. I finally put my bandana around my lower face bandit-style. This helped a lot, but the flies are very bothersome.

Day 128   *Sumner, Illinois*

Flies harassed me for over five hours today without let-up!

I'd hoped to stay at a B&B in Lawrenceville, but I had no luck with two places. So when I saw a sign for Red Hills State Park, I followed Yogi Berra's advice and took the fork in the road.

I'm now camped by a lake, waiting for the sun to pass over and for the day to cool off. At least I'm in my tent and protected from the flies.

I'll be entering Indiana tomorrow.

Today is Mother's Day, and that's whom I'm thinking about.

Vincennes, Illinois   Day 129

Some brilliant person decided that Hwy 50 should have rumble strips that run perpendicular to the road across the entire shoulder. For miles. Instead of making it just difficult to walk with a kart, why not make it next to impossible?

I stopped at the Marathon gas station store for breakfast, and Kay made two egg sandwiches for me. Later she told me she was 70 and worked 10 to 12 hours a day. "It's either that or stay home."

Later I met two angels-on-the-road. The first was Gary. When he opened his car window to chat, we were *both* enveloped in flies! He returned 20 minutes later, stuck his hand out, and gave me a container of "Dixon's Gotcha Covered" deet-free bug spray. I grabbed the lit-

tle bottle, shook his hand, and sprayed as I kept walking east. The spray did help a little.

An hour later a young woman in a Buick pulled up, got out of her car, and handed me a gift-bag containing snacks and two bottles of electrolyte and vitamin water. I gave Tracie my card and my sincere thanks.

When I crossed the Wabash River into Indiana, not only did the stupid rumble strips disappear, but so did the flies. *Hallelujah!*

My room tonight at the Holiday Inn was a gift from Ben Tarpley, one of my travel consultants, and a terrific guy. Thank you, Ben!

Day 130   *Washington, Indiana*

The heat continues. My head sweats. I wipe it off. Repeat.

I drink water all day long.

When I crossed the Wabash into Indiana yesterday I entered the Eastern time zone. This has an impact on how I plan my day.

Today I listened to a fun Marc Maron interview with Cheech & Chong. I loved their albums and movies. The story of how the two met is fascinating.

A package from Amazon was waiting for me when I checked into the motel today. It contained mosquito netting that I wished I'd had two days ago but no longer needed and two tubes of Benadryl anti-itch cream that I immediately applied to my bites.

One thing I've learned on this journey is that trying to plan more than a day or two in advance is senseless.

Now that the temperatures are again getting into the 90's and the humidity is high, I'm not sure I can force too many 25-mile days. It's just too exhausting.

Loogootee, Indiana   Day 131

Last night I dragged myself across the highway to Walmart and stocked up on soup, crackers, protein bars, and trail mix. I also bought a small container of cut-up melon. My body continues to crave fruit and vegetables.

Highway 50 is now a two-lane blacktop, with a shoulder just wide enough for the kart. The day was overcast, the temperature was comfortable, and the bugs were few.

A young woman named Molly stopped her car and handed me two bottles, one of water, the other of Sprite, and said she'd seen me earlier. I thanked her and invited her to follow my journey online. I hope she does.

I'd called the El Dorado motel in Loogootee earlier, and Lilly had saved a room for me. It's okay. Also, it's the only game in town.

Day 132

Martin State Forest, Indiana

I had a bad neighbor at the motel last night—I suspect drugs, alcohol, and/or mental health issues—so I listened to the sound of rain on my sleep app all night.

I found another wallet today. No cash but many cards, including Navy ID. About 20 minutes later I met Marie who was standing near her mailbox. She said she'd take care of the wallet and called the sheriff's office to report the find. She's obviously well-connected.

Soon I saw a sign for the Martin State Forest campsites.

"Do you know how far it is to the campsite?" I asked a park office employee as she drove by.

She said she'd drive there and check the mileage. When she returned a few minutes later, she said, "It's a sixth of a mile."

"You mean 'point-six'?"

"I guess, yes." Those darned fractions and decimal points are confusing. I thanked her and walked up and down some steep hills to the spot.

I was the only camper and enjoyed the solitude and sounds of nature.

Bedford, Indiana   Day 133

Rain was in the forecast, so I kept my rain gear handy. I was on the road at 6:30 a.m., with a long day ahead of me.

The first 10 miles was up and down winding hills. I often crossed to the opposite side of the road when there were blind turns up ahead.

At one point I arrived at a long stretch where one of the lanes was closed, and I was passed through by dozens of friendly construction guys.

Near Bedford it started to drizzle. I ducked inside Subway as the rain increased. As I waited to place my order, I chatted with Jerry, who insisted on treating me to lunch.

Teela and the rest of the crew wanted a photo with me. I told the store manager I'd be happy to be the new Subway spokesman.

It was raining heavily when I left, but 15 minutes later I checked into the motel and was soon soaking in the Jacuzzi.

Day 134   *Medora, Indiana*

At 2:30 a.m. I was awakened by loud voices coming through the adjoining door to the next room at the motel. At times like these I miss sleeping in my tent. Once again I changed rooms in the middle of the night.

After breakfast I walked to the Bedford post office where Cathy, the clerk, actually packed all the items I was sending home in a box and sealed it up while asking about my trip. It was the best post office service I've ever received in my life!

I walked through the beautiful countryside as it rained on and off all day.

For a while I sat and chatted with Shane, Brandon, Rachelle, and their goat, Gabby. Then I walked another few miles and saw a man who'd just taken the mail out of his mailbox.

"Excuse me," I called.

Larry Curry greeted me with a smile.

I described my situation and asked if he'd permit me to pitch my tent somewhere on his lawn for the night.

"Sure! Do you need an extension cord? Bottle of cold water?"

I chatted on the back porch with him and his son, Hunter. Larry operates heavy equipment, and Hunter, who's taking classes in medical billing and coding, loves to sing (he had supporting roles in four high school musicals, including *Grease* and *Cinderella*). More angels!

Seymour, Indiana   Day 135

In the morning, I thanked Larry for his hospitality, piled my tent (wet from dew and condensation) onto the kart, and got on the road. It was mostly downhill and there wasn't much traffic.

When I arrived at Brownstown, I walked into the Dairy Queen for some food or a shake. But the line was too long, so I left and got back on the highway, soon passing the county jail and the fairgrounds. A few miles later I realized I was on the wrong road. How had I messed up?

I doubled back and at the Dairy Queen I saw the answer—the Hwy 50 sign was blocked by the restaurant signage; I'd gone straight instead of making a left turn.

It was warm going for a long while.

Tonight I splurged on a "real meal" at Applebee's courtesy of Lu, a lovely woman from North Vernon who asked about my walk and then handed me a generous gift.

Artist of the Day: Bill Watrous, a phenomenal trombonist and, judging from his videos and solos, a fun guy.

I just weighed myself in the Holiday Inn fitness room. If you're interested in losing some weight, walk 2,000 miles.

Day 136 *North Vernon, Indiana*

This afternoon I set up my tent on the back deck of the home of Lu, whom I met yesterday on the road to Seymour. She and her husband Phil live in a lovely home in North Vernon with their Schnauzer, Jazzie.

When I spoke with Lu yesterday and discovered they lived close to my next destination, I asked about the possibility of camping in their yard, and she said yes.

I'm set up under a porch overhang in case of rain.

And sure enough, at 6:23 p.m. the rain started coming down. It's pouring! But hey, I'm dry.

Lawrenceburg, Indiana **Day 137**

Last night, Lu warned me about the challenges I'd be facing this morning—weather, road construction, detours, and poor highway conditions. She offered to give me a ride past the mess.

I've learned to pay attention when people who know the area well make a suggestion.

So this morning, Lu, Jazzie, and I piled into her vehicle, and she drove me to Dillsboro. On the way, we talked about how some people, including she, made assumptions about who I am and why I'm pushing a kart along the highway.

Lu said that while she and her husband had not worried about inviting me to stay in their backyard, she was warned by others that I might be a crazy person/rapist/axe-murderer. And she still knew little about me. (I filled in some of my life story; she seemed surprised.)

The walk from Dillsboro to Lawrenceburg featured plenty of road construction, but it did not affect me as much as the heat and humidity did.

The last few miles into town were exhausting, and I arrived drenched.

Day 138   *Cincinnati, Ohio*

I was happy to finally arrive in Cincinnati, where my son, Adam, lives with his wife, Kelly, and my grandson, Maxwell.

On my way to downtown Cincinnati, I passed through many old neighborhoods and villages along the Ohio River, which separates Ohio and Kentucky. Everyone I met along the way was friendly.

After walking 14 miles, I needed to detour to Adam's house, so I called Lyft. A friendly guy named Nick, a former financial advisor, drove me through the heavy downtown traffic.

It was great to see everyone! After dinner we went to watch Adam's adult softball league game. Soon the sun had gone behind the trees and a cool breeze picked up.

I'll be here three nights, but plan to put on some walking miles during the day while everyone's at work or school (except for the dog and the two cats). Cincinnati's a big city.

Cincinnati, Ohio Days 139–141

Day 139. There was no reason to walk on a highway today, but I still wanted to make some "progress." So the 14 miles I walked today I'll count toward my eastern progress.

I wish every day's walk could be as pleasant as today's. First, I passed through the Indian Hill neighborhood, filled with large homes on large grounds. Adam tells me many professional athletes and other wealthy Cincinnati residents live in this area.

I followed a sign directing me to the Little Miami Scenic River Trail. Originally a railroad track, it's been reclaimed for recreational use, similar to the Katy Trail but with asphalt paving. Much of the trail was in shade. The day was absolutely beautiful.

I'm convinced that now is the time to ship my kart and most of my stuff home and walk the remainder of my journey less encumbered. Sadly, motels are still few and far between; this is what makes cycling cross-country more feasible than traveling by foot.

I continued to the town of Loveland, where Adam met me for lunch at Paxton's Grill. I ordered portobello mushrooms with spicy hummus, some kind of soft cheese, and broccoli.

After lunch we went next door to Loveland Sweets, one of Adam's clients. (Adam is the owner of *WeGo Unlimited,* a growing web design, brand identity, and marketing solutions agency.) While he and the owner talked business, I had a cup of Girl Scout Mint Cookie ice cream. Incredible! The offerings are the stuff that makes candy store dreams a reality.

Day 140. This morning I had breakfast and headed back to Indian Hill. But today I turned right onto the Little Miami Scenic River Trail.

Walking 10 miles is good for thinking, and I'd made the decision to resume my walk to the Atlantic without my kart. The thought of pushing it 600 more miles on the hilly roads of West Virginia and beyond was a concern. I just hope my back, knees, and shoulders can tolerate the pack.

After several hours I ended up at the Growler Stop, a gas station and convenience store that's rebranded itself as a craft beer bar. I called Adam to pick me up while I ate one of their craft pretzels and a non-craft A&W Root Beer.

We drove first to Dick's Sporting Goods where I bought a backpack and a new pair of Merrell waterproof shoes. Then we went to REI where I purchased a bivy sack. It's smaller than a tent and much lighter. I'll probably be using it just a few times.

In the evening I took everyone out to Brown Dog Cafe for dinner. Kelly and I split a veggie pizza *and* a tasty veggie burger, with a side of vegetables. Afterwards, Adam treated us to frozen yogurt at Rhino's.

Day 141. It was Shabbat today, an appropriate day to rest and recover from the stress of the last few days, weeks, and months.

Adam and I brought both the 27-gallon container, which I'd separated from the kart, and the kart itself to the UPS store. I shipped the container home and sent the kart to my friend Ben, who is planning a journey of his own.

Later in the afternoon, we all went to see *Solo: A Star Wars Story.* It was entertaining, with plenty of chase scenes.

Tomorrow I begin the next phase of my journey, carrying instead of pushing.

A Visitation

It has taken me over 50 years to become comfortable telling this story. It was just too personal, and it exposed feelings that I could not easily share.

But after what I experienced on my journey across the country, the extreme heat and cold, the pain, the challenges and the risks, I look at life—and death—differently. Also, I care less and less about what people think of me. In fact, I really don't give a damn at all anymore about what people think of me. (It's quite liberating. You should try it.)

When I was 18 years old and had finished my first year of college, I became severely ill. I had ulcerative colitis. It's a condition no one knows too much about. No one knows the cause, and there's no effective cure. I'd had one serious bout earlier in my life, but I recovered then and expected to recover again. But I didn't.

So instead of going back to college, I went to Mt. Sinai Hospital in New York. I spent nine weeks there, getting blood transfusions, taking all manner of corticosteroids and other medications. I was in a lot of pain and most likely addicted to the Demerol they were giving me.

No one ever thought to weigh me, and one day as I slowly wandered down a hospital hallway pushing an IV pole on wheels, I saw a scale and stepped on it. I was shocked to discover I'd dropped from 125 to 95 pounds in the space of six weeks.

I was sick. Really sick. And more than that, I came to realize, I was dying. I could tell from the doctors' hushed conversations and the concerned looks of my parents that nothing but major colon surgery was going to save me. Maybe.

In a strange coincidence, it was around this time that I received a letter from the Draft Board informing me that because I was no longer enrolled in college, I'd lost my student deferment. I was now reclassified 1A and needed to report for a physical.

Like many hospital patients, I'd flipped day and night. I slept most of the day, waking only for visitors, meals, blood tests, and occasional sigmoidoscopies. I was awake much of the night in the dimly lit room, with the soft sounds of my radio tuned to an easy-listening station in the background, looking out the window, just drifting.

It was at such a moment in the earliest hours of the morning that I heard a quiet voice, or felt it really. The voice asked, simply, *"Are you ready?"*

I had no doubt what that meant. I was being asked to make a choice. I distinctly remember not being afraid. It was all very peaceful and calm. The greatest calm and peace I'd ever experienced.

I don't know how long I waited before responding, but I finally answered, "No."

And then the voice asked me, simply, *"Why?"*

After a minute or two I responded, "Because I'm too young."

And I did believe I was too young to die. I had my reasons. I had not yet had a satisfactory sex life. I hadn't finished college. I'd never been to Europe. That's what I remember thinking as I chose life over death.

And the voice said, simply, *"Okay."*

And that was that. When my doctor came in to see me the next morning, I asked him what it would take for me to get out of the hospital. I knew I needed to leave or I would die here. He laughed a skeptical laugh and told me I would need to put on weight. I asked how much. He was visibly surprised at my attitude. I was negotiating with him. He said 15 pounds. I agreed to the deal.

I became obsessed with gaining weight. I ate all day and night. I met with the hospital dietician, who approved anything I ordered for meals. At my request, my parents brought me boxes of chocolate donuts and gallons of whole milk (not the recommended diet for a person with UC, but who knew?). And I started to gain weight. I weighed myself constantly. When I'd put on 15 pounds, I demanded to be released. After a final blood transfusion, my parents drove me home. My impression was that the doctor was sure I'd die at home. My belief was that I wouldn't.

It took over a year to regain my physical strength. At first I couldn't climb stairs, and walking a few hundred feet was a challenge. I looked like hell because of the side effects of prednisone. I started my personal rehab by walking around the block. Later I borrowed a neighbor's bike and rode it for 5, then 10, minutes. I weaned myself off my meds. It was a

long, slow, painful, frustrating rehab period filled with more failures than successes. My first attempt to go back to college was a failure, and I came back home for another semester.

But in the end I did go back to Boston University. I changed my major from Business to Communication, went to summer sessions, and eventually graduated just one year late. I got married at 22 before my senior year, and after graduation I moved with my then-wife first to San Francisco, then to Oakland.

Many people call an experience such as I had "a visitation." For me, it was a confirmation that God not only exists, but cared enough about me to ask if I was ready.

Fifty years later I do not worry about death. In fact, I've *never* worried about death since that night. Let me state flatly and for the record that not having a fear of death puts you in a unique category.

But more than this, having once before been at that moment of truth where I could have gone either way, I am not convinced that the alternative would have been either a mistake or wrong. It just would have been different. I've caused friends to laugh when I've occasionally said, "Life is overrated."

Regardless, I can tell you this: I take life very seriously.

Some people feel that we're on borrowed time. But I do not. I view life as not only a gift and a blessing but as an obligation as well—an obligation to use the time you have to the best of your ability.

Having been given this gift, I don't abuse it, and I don't take unnecessary risks. I've pursued much of what life has to offer. And now I've walked across America, something few others have done.

And when people along the journey said to me, as they often did, "God bless you," I would smile, thank them, and know in my heart that God has, indeed, blessed me.

Hillsboro, Ohio   **Day 142**

I survived my first day carrying the backpack. It wasn't easy.

While 23 lbs. is not particularly heavy for a backpack, I'd never hiked any significant distance carrying that much weight.

My personal philosophy is this: if you can do one pull-up, you can do two; if you can lift 50 lbs., you can lift 60 lbs.; if you can walk 10 miles, you can walk 15. So if I can survive a 17-mile walk carrying a 23 lb. backpack, I can do it again tomorrow.

I had a good fish sandwich at the S & K Dairy Cup. I also had a chocolate malt reminiscent of those of my youth.

While eating, I chatted with Greg Youngstrom, an environmental scientist with the Ohio River Valley Water Sanitation Commission, which monitors the river's water quality.

After checking in at the Days Inn, I ate at the local McDonald's. I gave Regina, the shift manager, a card, and she offered me a free hot fudge sundae. I think I got the better part of that deal!

Day 143   *Bainbridge, Ohio*

Today I was able to give back after having received so much.

A long hike on a hot day brought me to Bainbridge, where I'd planned on staying at the Hirn House, a local B&B. But the owner's son has returned from college, so his room is no longer for rent!

The owner referred me to the local Methodist church, and I was given the okay to pitch my tent behind the Painted Valley Ministries Food Pantry.

Soon after I arrived there, Merri Thompson, who's in charge of the Pantry's food distribution, said I could stay inside overnight.

People were already lining up to receive a food box, and I asked if I could help. Without hesitation Merri put me to work, alongside Lana and Michelle, assembling dozens of boxes, each containing cereal, pasta, juice, spaghetti sauce, canned and fresh produce, and bakery items.

Although I've donated to a food bank through Temple Sinai's annual campaign, it was an honor and privilege to actually be on the front line helping to distribute the food. It was their gift to me.

Chillicothe, Ohio   **Day 144**

When I saw Merri before I left this morning, she asked, "How did you sleep?"

"About as well as I ever sleep."

This "quality of sleep" business is not something I truly understand. Any advice I hear or read that one should "get more sleep" is, to me, laughable. What, you don't think I'd *like* to sleep more? It doesn't always work that way. I figure, if I can function, I must have gotten enough sleep. But that's just me.

The last mile or two walking into Chillicothe was on a sidewalk. For a half mile prior to that it was on the narrow edge of a retaining wall.

I have no idea where I'll be the next few nights, and I'm still getting used to my backpack. Also, it's no surprise I'm again dealing with blisters.

Day 145

Athens, Ohio

After six hours of walking, I was having a helluva time trying to find a decent place to camp. Then it started to rain. At that point a man in a Prius pulled up and asked if I'd like a ride. Absolutely!

He was on his way to Athens, Ohio, and so was I. While I generally don't like to take rides, my feet were cheering.

Jim Fuller told me about his two careers—insurance agent and adjunct professor of business at Ohio University (my son Adam's alma mater).

When we got to Athens, Jim drove me around the impressive campus and then dropped me at my motel.

I later had a Skype conversation with my friends Bill Devore and Barbara Feinstein, both experienced backpackers and hikers, who confirmed that my backpack difficulties were more or less normal and I'd eventually overcome them.

All blisters are now taped with Leukotape K and will hopefully heal with time.

Parkersburg, West Virginia

Days 146–147

Seven miles out of Athens, I got caught in a sudden downpour of rain and hail, accompanied by thunder. By the time I had my rain jacket on, I was thoroughly soaked.

To avoid ticks, I'd tucked my pants into my socks, and the rain had run into my waterproof shoes. I was still 11 miles from my destination.

I took a moment to laugh at my situation and then walked across the grass median to the shoulder on the other side of the highway, which was wider.

A few minutes later a mid-sized Penske truck pulled over and offered me a ride. It was Ovidio, from El Salvador, delivering a load of vegetables.

When he asked me my name I replied, "Roberto." This pleased him. When I asked if I could take his photo, he said it was not a problem because he had a work visa.

We chatted in Spanish and English and enjoyed each other's company until he dropped me off in Belpre, Ohio.

The rain had stopped, and I walked several more hours (with wet feet) to a motel in Parkersburg.

Unfortunately, the room was not clean and smelled of smoke, and a wasp I tried to shoo from the room stung me (insect gratitude is an oxymoron). So I walked next door to the Red Roof Inn and got a much nicer room for the same price. The first motel processed a refund with no hassle.

I put my wet things in the dryer and took a shower. The sun came out and all was well in West Virginia.

You can't will your body to heal, but you can rest it. And that's what I decided to do today.

The blisters are still tender; hopefully they'll be a little better tomorrow. My shoes were damp so I used the hairdryer to blow-dry them.

I ordered in some comfort food for lunch—pizza with anchovies and mushrooms, salad, and cheesecake; I'll be eating the same thing for dinner.

It's been gray and gloomy all day. Regardless, I'm heading out tomorrow morning to resume this last stage of my journey.

Walker, West Virginia   **Day 148**

I was up early, wrapped my blisters in Leukotape K, packed my backpack, and walked onto Hwy 50 East—going the "wrong way."

Five hours later I stopped at Back Woods Pizza in Deerwalk, ate a pizza sub and a chocolate chip cookie ice cream sandwich, and drank a root beer.

A few miles later I walked into Mountwood Park.

The campsites were another two miles into the park. Forget that.

I looked behind a nearby wooden fence and discovered a concrete pad hidden behind it. Given the empty cartridges scattered around, it was obviously a shooting range—a perfect place to spend the night!

The night was warm and humid, and the sounds of birds and distant traffic filled the air. I was using the bivy sack for the first time.

Day 149

Ellenboro, West Virginia

I awoke after midnight to a sky filled with stars and many fireflies. It was a magnificent scene. After watching the flickering fireflies (and a few satellites passing by) through the screen in my bivy, I eventually fell back to sleep.

Sadly, camping in a bivy does have its downside. For example: extracting oneself from the sack to go pee in the middle of the night is a major production. Fortunately, it wasn't raining.

Leaving the park the next morning, I walked along the rolling West Virginia hills in the early mist for hours, taking frequent rests as I shifted the backpack and tried to ignore the intermittent blister pain in my right foot.

When I finally walked into the Sleep Inn, Benita greeted me warmly.

I stashed my gear and hobbled over to a nearby place for lunch.

Whenever I'm feeling sorry for myself, I think of the millions of refugees around the world seeking asylum, or of the hardships my grandparents endured as immigrants to this country. My "hardships" are nothing compared to theirs.

Virtually every day someone asks why I'm doing this, and I talk about my father and his World War II service. Compared to my dad's 44 missions in a B-24 bomber in the South Pacific, this is a cakewalk.

Salem, West Virginia　　**Day 150**

For miles and miles I had highway sounds on one side of me and freight train sounds on the other. I miss the trains.

Fortunately, the songs of many birds filter through the vehicle noise, and I concentrate on those.

At noon I stopped for lunch at a Sub Express and enjoyed having sliced mushrooms and sweet peppers on my tuna sub.

I eventually arrived at an RV park along Hwy 50. On the phone, the owner had said I could camp on the grass along the stream. He didn't mention money, and neither did I.

For several hours I hung out at the picnic table under a shade structure and rested, texted, and read. When no one paid any attention to me, I just set up my bivy right there. If it rains, I'm covered.

Later Garland came over and he told me about his family. Jim joined us and brought me two peanut butter sandwiches for the road. Each works in construction or for an oil crew, lives in his RV during the week, and travels home on weekends.

The people I've met along my journey are good. They work hard. They're generous.

Day 151

Bridgeport, West Virginia

As I walked through Clarksburg I was happy I wasn't pushing my kart. There's absolutely no shoulder at all, and the narrow border of grass is barely wide enough to walk on. That said, I miss what was *in* the kart—my tent; soup; extra water; the camp stool.

West Virginia is certainly beautiful. The trees, hills, and sky all are gorgeous.

When I left this morning, my bivy was wet from dew and condensation, and that's how I had to pack it. I encountered rain a couple of times today, but had my rain jacket handy.

I'm beginning to see the end in sight. Another few weeks. I can make it.

Today I chatted with Eric and his co-workers at a rest stop. The guys were young, friendly, and interested in my journey.

What I Learned Along the Way

You'll get blisters and they'll hurt. Then they'll turn into callouses and stop hurting.

If you're pushing or carrying too much weight, get rid of stuff.

They say if you want to hear God laugh, make plans. God hasn't stopped laughing since I took my first step. I'm still making plans, and God is still laughing.

The desert will kill you without a second thought. It defeated me, but it didn't kill me because of the intervention of friends and my desire to live.

Where I come from, just about the only time you hear anyone speak the word "God" is when you're sitting in a religious service or if someone sneezes. That's not the way it is in many of the 14 states I walked through.

Don't ignore angels. Some people will go out of their way to help you. Let them.

Most people have bigger problems than you do.

This country is not designed for walking. It's designed for driving. So when you're having a rough time walking coast-to-coast, it's not really your fault.

Route 66 may have been charming once, but it isn't anymore.

Pricier motels aren't necessarily better than cheaper ones. And motel soundproofing is an iffy thing.

I love to sit in the Jacuzzi.

The day goes best when you get a really early start. Especially when the temperature is heading upwards toward 100°F.

After walking and camping for weeks, your level of personal and food hygiene drops a few notches.

There's a knack to "relieving oneself" on the road. (A book has been written about it).

There are good cops. When you meet one, it renews your confidence in law enforcement.

There are no perfect shoes.

You never think about Indian Reservations until you're walking through one.

On any journey you must maintain a balance: time vs. miles-to-go.

Man and nature will throw impediments in your way.

There are definite limitations to your own physical and mental strengths. But often you can surprise yourself with your capabilities.

Sometimes you need to make quick decisions; other times you need to pause and think things through.

It would be nice to take a "day of rest" each week while you're on the road. But if you do, it will take you forever to reach your destination.

Some people think a journey such as this was fun. *("Cristoforo, I'm sure you'll have fun on your voyage.")* This was not fun. My wife and close friends will tell you that I don't understand the concept of fun. I just wanted to finish the damn walk and wade into the Atlantic.

I was advised not to say, "I'm attempting to walk across the country," and instead say, "I'm walking across the country." This did not work for me. I was *always* attempting to walk across the country until the moment I actually succeeded.

If I had known when I started what I know now ... Well, life doesn't work that way, does it?

Note—When I shared my list with my friend and fellow cross-country walker, Jeff Rudisill, he sent me his own list. Here it is:

Our fears and "stuff" keep us from living our lives.

Law enforcement personnel are good at telling you what you *can't* do, but are not as good at telling you what you *can* do.

Other than automobiles, there's very little to fear in the outdoors.

There are lots of good people in this country.

Our bodies and minds quickly adjust to our environment.

We should have long term goals, but work at them day-to-day.

Don't worry too much about things that might happen down the road; just get through each day.

Very few people have a good understanding of either distance or direction.

We are more committed to being comfortable than we are to being healthy.

We have to learn to receive as well as to give.

Fatigue overcomes fear.

We should share special things with special people.

Day 152

Fellowsville,
West Virginia

Highway 50 in West Virginia is mostly a long, winding, two-lane blacktop.

Fortunately for me, it's been cool and overcast, perfect for walking.

I sat for a while at a church picnic table and watched a road crew repaint the double yellow line down the middle of the road. There's not too much traffic, and the paint appeared to dry quickly.

At the Company's Comin' Diner, the best buckwheat pancakes in the world were served up by two ladies who reminded me of Aunt Bea. They're probably both my age.

A big red dog followed me for a while, and I had to chase it off. I'm adjusting to the backpack and walked 24 miles today.

I set up for the night on a side road behind a gospel church. The Internet connection was very weak, but I was able to send a text with my location to Sharon.

Aurora, West Virginia   Day 153

I walked down the hill, filled with hairpin turns, and stopped for breakfast at a roadside café. But the buckwheat cakes didn't compare to the ones I had last night.

As I approached the foot of the next climb, I met Tim, a scary-looking but otherwise pleasant guy with a half dozen dogs and two dozen vehicles in his yard. He warned me about the upcoming steep climb, but I told him I'd already walked over 2,000 miles so far and this wasn't going to stop me. I think he was skeptical.

It was a one-and-a-half-hour climb before the road leveled off. After that, the walk was easy.

Along the way I asked an older couple (i.e., my age) if they would fill my water bottle. Carolyn and Randy gave me some cold bottled water and a Cranberry Sprite and then invited me to join them for a peanut butter and Welch's grape jelly sandwich lunch. We discussed religion—they're Jehovah's Witnesses—and the economics, population, and geography of this part of West Virginia. Politics did not come up.

At 5 p.m. I spied an unoccupied pasture, snuck in, set up the bivy and, in order to avoid the flying insects, I got in for the night.

Day 154

Mount Storm, West Virginia

Today I was the kid in the story who had to walk six miles to school—*uphill both ways.*

Yesterday's climb was tough. Today's was even steeper—a 17-mile, hard-fought battle, and my feet are complaining.

The motel I'm in is, once again, the only game in town. I keep telling myself it's just for one night.

After walking in West Virginia for a couple of hours this morning, I passed into Maryland. Then, due to the vagaries of state borders, I was back in the hills of West Virginia.

Passing a friendly young man exiting his pickup, I asked if he had any extra water. Patrick, a service technician for NeuBeam, filled my bottles, and I complained about the lack of cellular service in the area.

"If you need to get online, just walk over to that building over there. I'll give you the password." There are all kinds of angels.

Romney, West Virginia Day 155

I have to admit I'm losing steam and limping along at this point. Both literally and figuratively.

This walk is not an easy undertaking, and my feet continue to pay the price. I have blue Leukotape K on eight of my toes.

This morning I hitched a ride down the hill with Carolina, a nurse from Indiana who's staying at the motel. I then proceeded to walk to the Koolwink, a retro, bright, and airy motel in Romney. I love it!

In spite of the beautiful scenery all around me, I still see the same stuff on the road that I've encountered from the first day—garbage, road kill, tools, vehicle parts, cans, and bottles. And discarded plastic. A simple "plastic recycling" web search will give you some idea of the problems we face.

I was humbled to read this today on Facebook:
Our Temple Sinai congregant and friend Robert Schoen is nearing the end of his walk across America. Follow him to get daily updates and to give him encouragement. I am in awe of this human being!
The reactions and supportive comments I get every day boost my spirits and help me walk another day. Thank you!

Day 156

Capon Bridge, West Virginia

It's raining again today. So I walked in the rain.

While I walked I listened to the conclusion of *John Quincy Adams* by Harlow Giles Unger. John Quincy was a noble character, extremely intelligent, well traveled, and knowledgeable about the world, languages, and political machinations. But sadly, he was not successful in his attempt to be "America's President." The Congress of his day was extremely polarized and thus ineffective. Not like it is now.

I'm trying out some different footwear. I have a pair of Reef "slides," which I wear at home all the time. They're great, and very comfortable. Although I've never done any serious walking in them, I figure I'd give them a try.

I found a place to set up the bivy under a picnic overhang.

Tomorrow I enter Virginia. (I can see it from here!)

Winchester, Virginia   Day 157

Today I had one of the most memorable experiences of my journey.

I was readjusting my pack during a downpour when a sheriff's deputy pulled up.

"Where you headed?" she asked.

"The Marriott in Winchester."

"Hop in, I'll drop you off." I opened the back door, got in, and sat back.

Ten minutes later she dropped me off under the Marriott's porte cochere. The rear doors of police cars can't be opened from inside, so the sheriff had to come around to let me out. Limo service at its most incredible! I thanked her, checked in, and headed to the Jacuzzi.

That evening, my friend Jeff Rudisill (who lives in Virginia) drove up and treated me to dinner at Applebee's. He's much tougher than I am, and never complains. I want to be like him when I grow up. We had a great time.

Later, I shared this photo with our mutual friend Ben Tarpley, who shared it on his Facebook page, writing:

"This is a photo of two gentlemen who each walked across America, but just met for the first time! While they come from different backgrounds and faiths (Jeff, a Christian, is holding a book authored by Bob, who is Jewish), they share a tremendous respect for one another. Each began his adventure AFTER reaching the age of 70. This suggests that most limitations are set by your mind and not your body."

Day 158   *Berryville, Virginia*

Before dinner last night, Jeff drove me to a nearby post office where I boxed up my camping equipment and sent it all home. Walking on the sidewalk out of Winchester this morning, it was almost a pleasure carrying my lighter pack!

Later, I had to travel on gravel along a narrow shoulder in heavy traffic for several miles. I shuddered at what it would have been like having to push my kart on that gravel path.

At last I reached the Historic Rosemont Manor, a quiet oasis with acres of lawns, trees, lovely décor, and tasteful furnishings. They were expecting me, and everyone treated me as if I were a celebrity.

The manor hosts many weddings, and I was reminded of the years I worked as a wedding bandleader. During my last few wedding gigs, I began to experience chest pains while playing the keyboard. Then the Great Recession came along and put an end to that career. Strange as it may seem, I never had chest pains before or since.

Loudoun County, Virginia

Day 159

After an enjoyable breakfast of a veggie omelet, veggie sausages, biscuits, and fruit, I said goodbye to the Historic Rosemont Manor.

Wearing my Reef slides with two pairs of socks, I walked in relative comfort and eventually arrived in Purcellville. There I treated myself to a chocolate malt at Market Burger. A few minutes later in walked my Wantagh High School classmate and kindergarten girlfriend Betty (Bladykas) Gleason and her daughter Kerry.

It was great to catch up on what's happened to us in the last 50 years. Betty lives in Florida but is in town for her grandson Ryan's high school graduation.

Kerry, her husband Daniel, Betty, and I went out for a really good pizza dinner. For dessert I ate a bunch of the terrific chocolate chip cookies baked especially for me by Betty.

I found a Sacagawea dollar on the road today. It's now my good luck piece.

Day 160   *Leesburg, Virginia*

If there existed a trail across the United States that was anything like the path I walked on today, people would be walking this county from coast to coast as if it were the Camino de Santiago or the Inca Trail.

The Washington and Old Dominion (W&OD) is an asphalt paved, converted Rails to Trails cycling/hiking path—I've walked on similar trails several times, most notably the Katy Trail. It's great! No trucks or cars, no non-existent shoulders, and no trash, either. Also, much of this trail is shaded.

After a while I left the path and walked into Historic Downtown Leesburg, which is quaint, charming, and filled with both locals and tourists. After lunch in a Chinese restaurant I continued walking through Southern Civil War history for several more miles.

Adding to the pleasant walk today was the pleasure of not having to carry my backpack.

Kerry and Betty picked me up after attending Ryan's graduation ceremony. In the evening we all went out to an enjoyable dinner.

Savage, Maryland   Day 161

Because I need to get to Annapolis by noon on Monday, I asked my hosts to drop me off this morning at Lock No. 10 on the C&O Canal Towpath in Cabin John, Maryland.

After saying a fond goodbye to Betty and thanking Kerry for her hospitality and for driving me all over the place, I walked along a gorgeous stretch of the Potomac River on the C&O Canal and Capital Crescent Trail. This is the same river in which President John Quincy Adams used to go skinny dipping (swim suits had not yet been created).

My destination was the DuPont Circle Metro station in Georgetown. Along the way I glimpsed the Washington Monument, a taste of sightseeing.

Christine Lee, my wife Sharon's dear friend, picked me up at the Metro station and drove me to her home in Savage. We had lunch on her back porch and enjoyed a long conversation. A few hours later Christine served up a terrific salmon dinner. I'm stuffed!

Silver Spring, Maryland, is where Sharon grew up. It's also where my daughter, Marna, lives with her husband and sons, and where I'm headed for the next two nights.

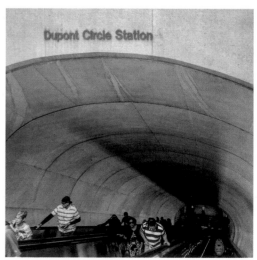

Silver Spring, Maryland
Days 162–163

Christine dropped me off at my daughter's home in Silver Spring at about 8:30 a.m. I said hello and goodbye to my son-in-law, Zak, and my grandsons Leo and Solomon, then left my backpack and headed out on the road to put in some walking miles.

The next couple of days are supposed to be warmer, so I want to get my walking in early.

Today's walk was, frankly, dull. Sidewalks, narrow shoulders, busy streets, strip malls and stores, city congestion, traffic lights, and noise.

As I walked I listened to Stanley Crouch's biography of Charlie Parker, *Kansas City Lightning,* and this made the miles more tolerable. It turns out that Bird and my father were both born in 1920. Parker died at age 34. (My father died at 96.)

After walking to Lanham, I took a Lyft back to Silver Spring.

Zak is a projection designer for theatrical productions. But he's also a bassist, and his older son Leo is learning the guitar. Leo and I jammed for a while on "Autumn Leaves," while Solomon (Solly), my youngest grandson, hung out. Marna is working late, so the guys and I went out to Subway for supper.

When she returned from work, Marna and I were finally able to spend some time together. It's not easy working two jobs and taking care of two boys. Both Marna and Zak have my sincere admiration.

The following morning, I saw Marna for a minute before I went out, putting in 10 miles on a walk to Bowie, Maryland.

Later we all went out for pizza and salad. Being with my daughter and her family to celebrate Father's Day is a particularly special treat for me.

Tonight I gave my first public talk about my journey to a group of Marna's co-housing neighbors. The questions asked form the basis of what I can expect in the future.

Annapolis & Grasonville, Maryland

Days 164–165

Although it was a hot, humid day today, I didn't mind. I wasn't walking. In fact, I spent most of the day in air-conditioned comfort.

Marna and I walked to the Silver Spring Metro Station, got on the same train car, and had a long conversation before I got off at Union Station. She continued on to work.

My Wantagh High School classmate, Gordon Peterson, soon picked me up at the station and we drove to Annapolis, where he treated me to lunch at the Severn Inn. Gordon, a US Naval Academy graduate, was a career Navy officer. He is a decorated Navy helicopter pilot and Vietnam war veteran as well as a former history teacher at the Academy. We've known each other forever.

The food at the Inn was excellent. After lunch, we shared two desserts.

Next up was a tour of Annapolis, a place he knows well. Memorial Hall is a sobering place. Bill Matthews, one of our Wantagh classmates, is memorialized on a plaque listing the 29 members of the Academy's Class of 1968 who were killed in the operational line of duty or combat. Billy, who died in a fighter crash in 1978, was well-liked and respected by all.

After visiting the tomb of John Paul Jones and the Navy Museum, we drove to a predetermined spot where I was transferred into the care of my good friends Ray and Marlene Parks.

Ray and I worked in an optical/optometry facility in Baltimore for three years before I moved back to California with Sharon in 1983. It was great to see them again, and we had a lot to catch up on as Ray drove over the Chesapeake Bay Bridge. We continued our discussion over dinner, their treat. I'm overwhelmed with everyone's generosity.

At this point I can taste the Atlantic Ocean.

Easton, Maryland

After breakfast this morning, I grabbed my backpack and out the door I went.

No rain today (good); it was mostly cloudy (very good); and for long stretches at a time I walked in the shade of trees along Hwy 50 (even better).

The highway is noisy, with two lanes of traffic in each direction. Regardless, this part of my journey provides a wide shoulder, which makes it all bearable. Also, I'm getting close to my goal. I'm counting down the miles, but I can't make them pass any faster.

Yesterday's excursion with Gordon to the Naval Academy and the time spent with Ray and Marlene provided a nice opportunity to rest up. All walks this coming week are on flat terrain and should be fewer than 20 miles a day.

Managers at both Choice and Wyndham Hotels have saved me money on several occasions by providing special discounts, and I appreciate it. Independent motels have also given me discounts, and at least once I was comped a room. I guess I'm a VIP!

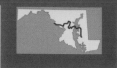

Cambridge, Maryland   Day 166

Each morning I head out on my journey hoping for no drama. I should know better. The drama finds me.

The Choptank River is a major tributary of the Chesapeake Bay. It runs for 71 miles. In 1985 the Markus Bridge replaced the Harrington Bridge. It's often called the Choptank Bridge. I don't know its exact length, but it's long.

I'd almost reached the eastern side when a black police car with lights flashing (no siren) pulled up in front of me. I was informed in a friendly manner by Cpl. Robbie Ball of the Cambridge, Maryland Police Department that pedestrians were not permitted on the bridge.

I didn't know, but the way things are, I wasn't surprised.

Then he told me that he would drive me over.

"But that means you have to drive all the way back!" I was surprised.

"Well," he replied with a smile, "I can't back up!"

So once again I found myself in the back seat of a police car. After making a U-turn at the end of the bridge, he deposited me where I'd been headed.

What could I say other than *Thank You!*

So You Want to Walk Across America

The estimates I've heard about how many people walk across the United States each year leave me skeptical. Maybe it's 20 a year. Or a dozen. Or perhaps fewer than five. There's no registry I know of. If you search Wikipedia, the list of people who have completed the trip numbers fewer than 40. That's nonsense. I can name five people off the top of my head who have completed the trip but aren't on that list. To get onto the Wikipedia list requires "media validation" and jumping through hoops that many successful coast-to-coast walkers won't see as worth it. Not everyone cares about being on "a list." *They* know they did it and probably don't care about proving anything to anyone. Each walk is different. There is no magic route. I know this, because I tried to find it. You're on your own out there, folks, and maybe that's what makes it magical.

Even the infamous American Discovery Trail— the cross-continental trail to end all trails—is no "walk in the park." The ADT is over 2,000 miles *longer* than most of the more direct routes across the country. It can often be inhospitable and is not always as accessible as one might hope. When I asked about pushing my walking kart on certain portions of the ADT, I was told it would not be possible; it passes through a number of state and national parks on hiking trails that couldn't accommodate my kart. That said, the ADT is certainly a viable route if you plan to carry a backpack, are willing to cache water and supplies, and don't feel like walking in traffic or on highways. As always, do your due diligence.

Before attempting to walk over 2,500 miles,

you should have a good conversation with yourself as well as with your doctor. I visited mine, both before and after my journey. While you'll get stronger as you progress, you still need to be in relatively good physical condition at the start and willing to endure real hardships on the road. You'll be facing serious heat, cold, wind, rain, and possibly snow, as well as insects, dogs, and a lot of oncoming vehicles.

A list of the items I brought with me or acquired along the way is included at the end of this book. I actually used many of the things I brought with me!

I can attest from personal experience that the great majority of people you meet along your journey will be kind, generous, caring, and helpful. Many strangers reached out to me with food, water, cash, shelter, and offers of rides during rough times on the road. But let's face it: I'm your average white male, somewhere between 18 and 80. If you fall into another category, your mileage may vary. And of course, not everyone you meet is going to be wonderful— there are some people out there who are nuts, jerks, or angry at the world.

Be prepared to sleep in locations you'd never dream of. American motels, road houses, B&Bs, lodges, hostels, and campsites are not situated at regularly spaced intervals as they are in many European countries. Apps such as warmshowers. com and couchsurfing.com may not work as well for walkers as they do for cyclists, although I met two wonderful families through these sites.

Two thousand miles of roads I walked along were bordered by barbed wire, and very often trees or bushes 20 feet beyond the fence that would have provided perfect opportunities for stealth camping, as well as protection and camouflage from the highway traffic, were not accessible. Finally, you can often travel hundreds of miles with little or no shade to protect you from the sun.

Prepare to ascend to elevations over 6,500 feet

and climb up and down steep hills for days at a time. Many if not most US highways offer little or nothing in the way of a shoulder to walk on. When you do find an adequate shoulder, count your blessings, since it will end abruptly when you least expect it, and you'll be back walking on sand, gravel, or the highway itself. Often there will be nothing except your wits and agility to protect you from oncoming trucks and cars often traveling at 75 mph. While most drivers— particularly truck drivers—are courteous and will often change lanes to avoid getting close to you, they don't always have that option because of traffic coming toward them.

To me, the most unpleasant aspects of walking across the country are the roadsides littered with all manner of garbage and debris. Plastic, glass, and metal bottles, cans, and cups; paper, plastic and foil food wrappers; leftover containers; plastic bags and drinking straws; car parts; toys; baby strollers; books; smashed computers, cell phones, cables, and CDs; road kill; used diapers, tampons, and condoms; pens and pencils; and every type of tool known to man can be seen along the roadsides. Work gloves, sweatshirts, blankets, pants, boots, shoes, flip flops, socks, wallets, backpacks, weapons, sunglasses, fishing lures and rods, hats, caps, bats, and balls of every type line the shoulders. It's not only a disgrace, it's a travesty.

Every walker shares common experiences, but each has unique experiences as well. One thing for sure, you will come to the attention of law enforcement. If you're not breaking the law, you'll probably be okay. The sheriff and local police officers were all courteous and concerned about my safety and twice gave me rides—once during a severe rainstorm and another when I had to cross a bridge where pedestrians are prohibited. The only time I was admonished—and given a written citation—was when I was walking on an Interstate highway (I was "guilty with an explanation"). After that, I avoided all

Interstates (making my journey much more complicated at times).

Depending on your route, you'll find that you may need to carry enough food and water for three, four, or even five days. Services on certain roads and highways can be nonexistent for a hundred miles or more. Often what's served at the gas station convenience stores you encounter is not something you'd ordinarily eat. (I hadn't eaten chicken for 25 years before my own walk but resorted to eating canned chicken noodle soup in an effort to obtain sufficient daily protein and nutrients.)

People who know and care about you will worry. And while you'll probably want to blog, use social media, phone home, check the weather, or listen to streaming podcasts, there will be long stretches where there is no internet connectivity. Having an external battery for recharging is a must.

Although you may plan your route in advance down to the smallest details, I guarantee these plans will change because of forces outside your control. Traffic accidents, road construction, weather, illness, and so many other things will come up. Even if it's not in your nature, you must be flexible. And as I've written elsewhere, whether you like it or not, you will be practicing mindfulness constantly. You have no choice. "Tomorrow" is just a concept when you've walked on the road for 23 miles dodging traffic while searching for a decent place to camp for the night.

Even if you've never walked 20 or 25 consecutive miles before, in time you'll get used to it. My job was to walk seven to nine hours a day—without overtime pay. And that will be your job, too, come rain or come shine.

It helps to be able to laugh at yourself. While I don't recall actually crying, I considered it several times. Groaning, cursing, and talking to yourself helps.

I found that whenever I hit a wall, a previously

invisible door opened up. An angel came to the rescue. Or the Sheriff's Deputy offered me a ride in the rain to my motel a few miles away, then opened the rear car door for me (since it couldn't be opened from the inside). Or a couple stopped to offer me money for lunch because they initially thought I was homeless, and later invited me into their home for shelter and conversation. There is no end to the angels you meet on the road.

Along the way, I learned one of the most important lessons in life: While it may be better to give than to receive, it's equally or more important to learn how to receive with grace and humility. And if you should be crazy enough to attempt a walk across America and succeed in doing so, be aware that the ending can feel quite anticlimactic. You may feel no great rush of success or accomplishment. Rather, a mixed feeling that while you know it's over, the reality of it all is elusive. Even while friends and relatives offer wishes of congratulations for the amazing feat you've performed, there is a certain empty feeling that takes weeks to dissipate. In the weeks following the completion of my coast-to-coast walk, as my feet healed and I re-entered the life I had left for half a year, I pieced together the experiences, the anecdotes, the acts of kindness, the moments of generosity shown me, the highs, lows, heat and cold, and tried to make sense of it all. Even now, months later, I'm not sure I can.

When someone close to me asked how the journey had changed me, my reply surprised even me. "I haven't changed; I'm just more the person I've always been."

Anyone who thinks walking across the country is about walking, I'm here to tell you that it's not.

Vienna, Maryland   Day 167

Hot, humid, and uneventful describes my walk to Vienna. My clothes, backpack, and I are all drenched with sweat.

The Tavern House Bed and Breakfast on River Road in this colonial town is charming. Located on the Nanticoke River, Vienna was founded in 1706.

My hosts, Elise and Harvey Altergott, are also charming as well as knowledgeable, well-traveled, and hospitable. Originally from Wisconsin, Harvey is an Annapolis graduate and former Navy pilot. Elise is from Massachusetts and worked in nursing and then electronics. They've run this B&B for over 30 years. And wow, it is *so quiet* here!

After a shower, I had a pleasant conversation with them during lunch in a lovely front room. I'm now resting in one of the five guest bedrooms. Tonight I'm the only guest, which is fine with me.

Tomorrow I'll be in Salisbury, one of the last stops in my journey.

Days 168–169

Salisbury, Maryland

Rain. Wind. Gray skies. I've seen worse of each, but I am nearing the end.

This morning's meal was epic. I counted eight varieties of fresh fruit and five different vegetables in a stunning variety of colors. Elise waved off my compliments, alluding to what she used to do in "the old days." (My "no meat" request eased her burden. That said, last night's snack included herring *and* sardines!) But on a sad note, she admitted that I might be their final B&B guest—age and memory issues were taking their toll.

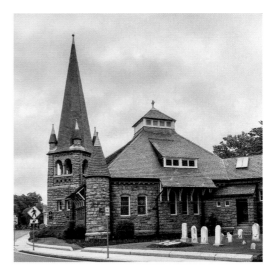

In the morning Elise and Harvey insisted on driving me to the other side of the Nanticoke River Bridge, where we said our goodbyes.

I walked into Salisbury, encountering heavy traffic and a plethora of fast food restaurants, gas stations, muffler shops, chain drug stores, a Walmart, strip and shopping malls, and congestion of every type. It rained on and off all day.

I spent the first night in a motel after waiting hours for clean linens. ("They're being laundered.")

The next day I took a five-mile walk through "Old Salisbury" and then checked into a better motel. After dinner, I spent my final night in Maryland.

Rehoboth Beach, Delaware

Day 170

This morning I'm headed to Rehoboth Beach to complete my journey.

Although I'd originally planned to walk directly from the Chesapeake Bay Bridge to the ocean, that's not how the cards fell.

Looking at the map, I realized that the distance from the Bay Bridge to Salisbury is virtually the same as the distance from the bridge to Rehoboth Beach. Whether this was a coincidence or divine intervention, I decided that I'd walked enough.

My Boston University classmate, Roger Passarella, picked me up in Salisbury and after a Swedish pancake breakfast at IHOP, we drove to Rehoboth

Roger dropped me off on the highway and, on an absolutely beautiful day, I walked the last couple of miles to the beach.

I strolled past the boardwalk, took off my shoes and socks, waded in, and ...

Poof! My journey is over!

Epilogue

Chadwick Island, New Jersey— Oakland, California

After I communed with the Atlantic Ocean, Roger and I took the Cape May–Lewes Ferry to New Jersey.

While I was standing on the upper deck of the ferry, a young man asked if I was a runner.

"Why do you ask?" I laughed. I'm definitely *not* a runner.

"Because you're built like a runner."

I told Tim, who's a Phys. Ed. teacher, that I'd just walked across the country. Now it was *his* turn to laugh.

I chatted with Tim and his partner, Julie, during the rest of the trip.

When we landed, Roger and I shared a pizza and beet salad in a local restaurant and then drove to his Jersey shore home on Chadwick Beach Island.

I spent the next two nights with Roger and his wife, Clare, just resting, recovering, eating, and walking on the beach and boardwalks.

Then Roger drove me to Newark Airport and I boarded a nonstop flight to San Francisco. I'd used 60,000 United miles for a business class seat. I wasted no time telling the flight attendant about my journey and my dad and asked if she'd give my card to the captain. Instead, she invited me to follow her to the cockpit and introduced me.

After meeting the captain and co-pilot and telling them about my father's service in the Army Air Force, I returned to my seat, sat back, relaxed, and enjoyed the best transcontinental flight I'd ever experienced.

My wife Sharon and several friends surprised me at the airport, and we all took BART (the Bay Area's public transit system) back to Oakland.

It was great to be home!

Final Thoughts

Today is the day after I completed my journey. All day I've thought about this strange emptiness I'm feeling. I'm not sure why, but here are some possible reasons:

1. I no longer have to wonder where I'll be sleeping tonight. (In a motel? Or a cow pasture? Behind a pile of asphalt? Beside a barbed wire fence? In someone's backyard?)

2. I don't have to worry about drinking water and certainly don't have to carry three gallons in my kart or two liters on my back.

3. I no longer need to consume 3,000+ calories a day or carry protein bars and packs of tuna.

4. I can finally stop looking at Google maps.

5. I don't have to photograph this morning's sunrise, the road ahead, or strange and unexpected objects I see on the side of the road.

6. And I no longer have to walk on narrow shoulders along the edge of busy highways, dodging trucks and cars, and worrying about blind curves looming up ahead.

Suddenly life is less intense; the environment is less intrusive.

For some reason, I've always been skeptical of the concept of "mindfulness" and the insistence that one has to "practice" it. As a result of my 170 days on the road, I truly believe that we live mindfully when we're called on to do so. At this point, my feeling is, "Why worry about being in the present if you don't need to?" In fact, having been forced to live in the present for so long, I can tell you that it feels good to once again be living in the past and the future.

And my body is quickly getting the message that it no longer needs to process everything I fuel it with (e.g., Snickers, fried fish sandwiches, French fries, root beer, and ice cream). It can just store it as fat.

This morning, after a late breakfast of oatmeal, fruit, and an outrageously good jelly donut, I walked for an hour on the boardwalk with my college friend, Roger Passarella. It was an easy stroll, especially after getting to the point where I can walk pretty much all day with only minimal breaks, which became my style of walking and contrasts with other hikers who take strategic breaks every two hours or so. It won't be long before I lose this ability (as well as the blisters and callouses that resulted).

The lesson to be learned is that the human body is capable of incredible feats given the opportunity.

So many people I met told me, "I could never do what you're doing!" But they're wrong. Many could. Not all, of course. But reaching for the inner strength to achieve a difficult goal is an innate human quality.

That's what I've come to believe.

What I Took on My Journey

Camping

Kelty Salida 2 tent with rain fly and footprint (a perfect tent for me and my stuff)

Outdoor Research Helium Bivy (this replaced the tent after Cincinnati)

Therm-a-Rest NeoAir air mattress (vital for your comfort)

Kelly Cosmicdown 20 sleeping bag (an excellent bag)

Neckbone pillow and small pillow case

Tom Bihn Daypack (whenever I left my kart someplace, my Daypack stayed with me)

LifeStraw personal water filter (I never used it)

Purification tablets (in the first aid kit; never used since I carried sufficient water)

Backpack (purchased in Cincinnati; it wasn't very good, the seams were splitting, and I returned it to Dick's Sporting Goods after returning home)

Clothing

Tilley Airflo hat (a great hat for protection from the sun)

Quick-dry Gadiemkensd baseball cap

2 pair Darn Tough cushioned hiking socks (these are great)

2 pair Injinji Outdoor Midweight Mini-Crew Socks (maybe they'll work for you)

2 eBags for clothing (kept things organized)

2 pair Columbia cargo pants, quick dry

1 pair convertible cargo pants; just the tops (I used them in the Jacuzzi)

REI silk long underwear

Long-sleeved Merino wool pullover (priceless)

2 pair Ex-Officio boxers (quick dry)

2 white Hanes Cool-Dri long sleeved shirts (protection from the sun; inexpensive)

1 Bandanna (protected me from the flies)

Patagonia jacket (lightweight and warm)

Columbia fast-dry long sleeved shirt (for dress up—I wore it once)

2 Nike fast-dry short sleeved athletic shirts

Marmot Pre-Cip rain jacket and pants

Gordini Polar gloves (the best)

Eddie Bauer Thinsulate gloves (useless; I sent them home)

Kippah (I almost used it once)

Minus33 merino wool beanie (wore this when it was cold and often for sleeping in the tent)

Web belt (canvas, military style)

Reef slides (flip-flops)

Teva sandals

Two pair walking shoes, one pair waterproof (I mostly used Merrells)

Food & Beverage

3 or 4 one-gallon plastic containers of bottled water

2 1.2-liter 45° SS vacuum water bottles

3 bottles of Gatorade (until I drank them up)

Almonds

Peanuts

Raisins (I ate peanuts and raisins all day long)

Dried apricots

Honey (I got rid of this after the ant episode)

Swiss cheese

Peanut butter (both organic and hydrogenated varieties)

Multivitamins and fish oil supplement (kept me lubricated)

Crackers (Wheat Thins and Triscuits)

Packs (not cans) of tuna (I always carried at least three packs)

Mustard

Toiletry & Hygiene

Toilet kit case

REI Backpacker Weekend First Aid Kit (don't waste your money)

Wahl Peanut hair/beard trimmer (later replaced by:)

Philips Norelco Beard Trimmer BT1217/70 USB rechargeable

Insect repellent

Sunscreen SPF 55 (used every day religiously)

Medium pump container of hand sanitizer (very important on the road)

Moleskin (overrated)

Leukotape K (used all the time; *much* better than moleskin)

Roll of paper towels

Toilet paper (later replaced by generic baby wipes)

Trowel

Generic Flonase (after a while I didn't need it anymore; resumed using at home)

Saline rinse packets and syringe (in the event of a cold or sinus infection, which never happened)

Knee support brace (used it for a few days; it helped)

Microfiber travel towel (if you don't have one, you'll need it)

Triple antibiotic ointment (aka: Aunt Evie's boo-boo cream)

Vigamox ocular antibiotic (expired in 2011)

Bar of Irish Spring soap (you'll be happy you have it)

Cortisone cream

Benadryl Extra Strength itch-stopping cream (a God-send)

Afrin

SPF lip moisturizer (needed this in the desert)

More insect repellent

Vaseline

Deodorant (useless)

Toothbrush

Toothpaste

Dental floss (every day)

Nail clippers

Cough medicine with codeine (never used)

Pain pills (used regularly)

Lorazepam (used as needed)

Cepacol throat lozenges

3 disposable razors

Tweezers

Tools & Electronics

iPhone 7+

12" MacBook with protective carrying sleeve (in the Daypack)

Titanium spork

An adjustable trekking pole (ostensibly to ward off dogs)

Sport-brella swiveling sun umbrella (used it in the tent for a while; then I gave it away)

Coleman Rambler II camp stool (invaluable)

Crescent wrench

Duct tape (if you don't have this, you'll need it)

Tripod (I gave it away)

Selfie Stick (too much trouble)

Plastic container for miscellaneous items

Power cord and USB cable assortment (in the Daypack)

Mophie XXL external battery pack (a must-have)

Anker 60W 6-Port USB Wall Charger PowerPort 6 (get one like this)

Dizaul solar battery (because I had the Mophie XXL, I never needed this)

LE power zoom flashlight (really bright!)

Pink Sharpie (I found it, then I lost it)

Rhodia notebook

Pentel pencil

Ballpoint pen (also served as potential deadly weapon)

Bungee cords (several sizes; the flat ones work best)

A book of matches featuring the image of LBJ

Victorinox Swiss Army Knife (works for the Swiss)

Leatherman Squirt multi-tool

Miscellaneous

Walker, my Runabout kart—with a 27-gallon container mounted on top

Bear/pepper spray (I almost used it once, but not on a bear)

Freemove safety vest (prevents drivers from running you over)

Yamaha piccolo (I sent it home after 2 weeks)

Business cards featuring my photo, a map of my journey, and social media info (you won't need 1,000)

Wallet with cash and a variety of credit cards

Postage stamps and a few envelopes

Polarized prescription sunglasses (*always* get polarized sunglasses!)

Two pair of prescription eyeglasses

National Parks Pass (I walked into one park but did not need the pass)

(Note: After walking 2,000 miles, I arrived in Cincinnati. At that point I switched to a backpack containing only essential items and sent everything else home.)

Acknowledgments

Think about it. A person cannot walk across America for 170 days, covering 2,644 miles, without support from home and help along the way. I was blessed with assistance virtually every day from a wide range of friends, relatives, and strangers. Some fed me, others housed me, many provided friendship and encouragement, some primarily worried about me, and a special few helped save my life. While I don't know the names of all the wonderful people who assisted me along the my journey, here are some of them:

Bronson Hamada, O.D.; Jeff Rudisill; Ben Tarpley; Scott McGaha; Deanna Nim & Walter Heuler; Officer Fabio Minoggio, Officer Jack Goins, and Chief Francis E. Bradley, Sr., Hualapai Police Dept.; Lisa Monheit; Father Mark Bertelli and Mary Agre, St. Mary of the Valley Church; Jeannine Smith; Naomi Theodor; Amanda & Troy Carmody; Jerry Houck & Ed Carr; Georgianna Lacey; Bailey Dunlap; Deborah Mendelsohn and Clayton at the Simpson Hotel; Weston Lee; Robert (Skip) Williams; Dharmesh, Shilpa, Aahana, and Aarav Bhakta; Sandra & Antonio Ortiz, and Antonio Jr.; David Locke; Bill Hext; Martha & Percy Brown; Jana Brown; Eric, Angela, Thaddeus, Declan, Bella, and Abigail Hanlon; Officer Reddy, Kansas Highway Patrol; Timothy Crawford, D.M.D.; Carina Guajardo; Rick & Tina Callahan; Todd & Sharon Peach; Sue Goodman; Rodney, Leanne, Kaleb, & Marcus Kasitz; John & Deb Mitchell; Ron Gossen; Bruce & Susie Tippit; Gerry Mandel; Sam & Trupti Patel; Jane Sweet; John Bayler; Debbie Greenwood; Hunter Curry; Larry Curry; Adam, Kelly, and Maxwell Schoen; Greg Youngstrom; Regina Blevins Hatch; Bruce Aiken; Meredith Thompson; Lu & Phil Wick; Jim Fuller; Ovidio Mancia; Bill Devore & Barbara Feinstein; Joshua Derry, General Manager of the Sleep Inn; Eric Stephens; Patrick Berrang at NeuBeam; Carolina Wurschmidt; Betty Gleason; Kerry & Daniel Thomas; Christine Lee; Marna Schoen; Zachary, Leo, and Solomon Borovay; Gordon Peterson; Ray & Marlene Parks; Cpl. Robbie Ball, Cambridge, Maryland Police Dept.; Elise & Harvey Altergott; Will Adams; and Roger & Clare Passarella.

Then there are the folks whose last names I don't know: Karen at Fisherman's Retreat, Redlands, CA; Chad, John, Juan, and Bill—everyone at the Monument Bar & Grill, Morongo Valley, CA; Robin, Terry, and Hunter at the Katy Bike Rental Shop, Defiance, MO; Rebecca at Pop-A-Wheelie Café, Defiance, MO; Sheryl & Vance at the

Seiling Motel, Seiling, OK; Rocky at Twin Pine Motel, Tipton, MO; the terrific Subway staff, and Cathy at the Post Office in Bedford, IN; Jubin at the Four Winds Motel, Carrizozo, NM; Reuben at the Bel-Air Motel, Vaughn, NM; Doug at the Barn B&B, Bluffton, MO; Joe at Hunter Heirloom Quilting Store, Warrensburg, MO; Becky and Luke at Backcountry Edge, Manheim, PA. And all the other wonderful people along the way whose names I may not recall, but I'll never forget your kindness.

Finally, there are special thanks due to my sister, Eve Samet, worrier-in-chief; Catherine deCuir, my talented music and writing partner; James & Pamela Au Photography—Jim and Pam, this would not be the same project without your talent, energy, and expertise; Linda Ronan, our wonderfully talented book designer; the great people at Stone Bridge Press, who brought the chronicle of my journey from concept to reality; Rabbi Jacqueline Mates-Muchin—obviously your blessing on the eve of my departure worked!; Cantor Ilene Keys, we always share a song in our hearts; Josh Bettenhausen, my tech guy, friend, and advisor—thank you. And my wife, Sharon Chabon, who has supported, cared for, and tolerated me for so many years, and gave me the go-ahead to begin and complete this once-in-a-lifetime journey.

About the Author

Robert Schoen is the author of the award-winning book *What I Wish My Christian Friends Knew About Judaism* and the co-author (with Catherine deCuir) of the novel *The Rabbi Finds Her Way*. He is a musician and has served as Composer-in-Residence at Temple Sinai in Oakland, California. Dr. Schoen, a retired optometrist, lives in Oakland with his wife, Sharon.